Guide to North Ameri

CABOOSES

Carl R. Byron with Don Heimburger

Kalmbach
Media

Don Heimburger grew up in central Illinois watching both Wabash and Illinois Central freight and passenger trains roll through his hometown. He is an editor, publisher, writer, and photographer with a specialty in prototype and model railroad communications, having owned and operated Heimburger House Publishing Company for 57 years. He earned a degree in journalism from the University of Illinois and has extensive experience in newspaper, magazine and web-based writing. He was Illinois Central Gulf's press representative, and also worked in public relations for a large Chicago-based financial association. This is his 14th book project.

Carl Byron's interest in trains started in the early 1950s, standing with his Dad at the Boston & Maine station in Shelburne Falls, Mass., as FTs and E7s (not to mention the streamlined *Minute Man*) rolled their trains past. (And an American Flyer set for his 5th birthday didn't hurt.) He graduated from Lowell (Mass.) State College in 1972 and remembers well that the campus abutted the B&M main line. Carl is a charter member of the B&M Railroad Historical Society and has written often for their *Bulletin*. He was a regular contributor to *S-Gaugian*, has written for *Classic Trains* magazine, penned *The American Streamliner*, *Volumes 1* and *2* and *The Pioneer Zephyr* with Heimburger House Publishing, and authored five volumes on New England railroading for Morning Sun Books.

Kalmbach Media
21027 Crossroads Circle
Waukesha, Wisconsin 53186
www.KalmbachHobbyStore.com

Published in 2021
25 24 23 22 21   1 2 3 4 5

Manufactured in China

ISBN: 978-1-62700-833-4
EISBN: 978-1-62700-834-1

Editor: Jeff Wilson
Book Design: Lisa Schroeder

Library of Congress Control Number: 2020940429

On the cover: Wide-cupola cabooses were designed to give crews better views of the taller cars and loads that were becoming common by the 1950s. Here Chicago, Burlington & Quincy 13606, built by International Car Co. in 1964, rolls behind a piggyback train in August 1966. The CB&Q would eventually have 125 such cars from International.
Chris Burritt; Don Heimburger collection

Back cover: Great Northern caboose X52 was built at the railroad's St. Cloud, Minn., shops in 1962. The standard cupola steel caboose is making one of its first road trips as it passes through Fargo, N.D., in August 1962.
Russ Porter; Don Heimburger collection

Contents

Gone but still an icon

Even though it's been gone from mainline railroads for more than 30 years, the caboose remains an icon of railroading. For more than 130 years, virtually every freight train in North America was trailed by a caboose. More than just a symbol or a vital center of operations, the caboose was, for many in the public, a human connection to railroads: A friendly wave from the conductor or brakeman on the platform or in the cupola window was the period at the end of the sentence as a train rolled past.

The caboose was replaced in the 1980s and '90s by the end-of-train device—that blinking, automated box known as an EOT or EDT—which continually monitors brake-pipe pressure and can send and receive information and commands from the head end. The rear-end crew is gone: the conductor moved to the locomotive and the brakeman position was eliminated or likewise moved forward; crew size was reduced from four to three or two. Railroads saved millions of dollars annually by eliminating the caboose, but at the price of becoming more distant and impersonal.

Although a few cabooses remain in service, mainly as platforms and shelters for crews during switching, transfer, and reverse moves, the days of cabooses on mainline freight trains have long since passed.

The loss of the caboose stirred strong emotions among those who follow railroading, with outcries rivaling the demise of steam locomotives. Other than locomotives, cabooses captured the interest and attention of railfans and modelers more than any other element of railroading, and although they won't be coming back, we are fortunate that many photographers documented cabooses and their operations throughout the 20th century.

The goal of this book is to show the tremendous variety of cabooses that ran on North American railroads: wood and steel; four-wheeled and eight-wheeled; short and long; with bay windows and cupolas; old and modern. We'll look at how cabooses evolved

This Erie caboose, with markers lit, rear door open, and interior lantern alight, gives life to the end of a stopped eastbound oil train during World War II. A westbound, headlight glowing in the distance, approaches for a meet. *Erie Railroad*

over time, see what caboose crew members did, how their duties evolved, and how cabooses played a role in train and railroad operations.

You'll see caboose photos from a variety of railroads as we examine many common designs, variations, and details. Although space precludes providing detailed roster and class information for all railroads, fortunately for railfans and modelers alike, dozens of excellent books have been published that focus on cabooses of individual railroads (and sometimes individual caboose classes). Many magazines and historical societies have published extensive articles including history, construction, drawings, and paint and lettering schemes (several historical sites and individual railfans have posted information online as well).

And now, sit back, turn the page, and enjoy an extensive tour of the world of cabooses. As you travel back in time, you'll gain a deeper understanding of how this symbol of railroading continues to endure.

Chapter 1

Caboose

FROM MODIFIED BOXCARS TO ROLLING OFFICES AND HOMES-AWAY-FROM-HOME

history

The "little red caboose" was an icon of railroading for more than a century. Colorado & Southern wood caboose 10592 brings up the end of a freight train heading out of Denver, Colo., in September 1965. The cupola window and rear door are open to provide ventilation on this late-summer day. The markers (lanterns) hanging at the rear corners are what officially indicate the end of the train: red lenses displayed to the rear; green to the sides. *Chris Burritt; Don Heimburger collection*

The little red caboose was an icon of North American railroading for more than a century, and it was an icon of Americana as well: *The Little Red Caboose* remained on many a preschooler's reading list for decades. Like the steam locomotive that preceded it into history, the caboose has a secure place in our lexicon and heritage.

The caboose's place in history was firmly secured both by its lengthy existence and constant visibility. The caboose rolled the rails for some 160 years, and—in a limited sense—still continues on. Its presence was universal and predictable. From the 1840s until the 1990s virtually every freight train in North America had a caboose marking its end. The railroad industry's Book of Rules defines a train as a group of cars with a locomotive and displaying markers at the rear (otherwise, it was just a group, or cut, of cars). The caboose was ubiquitous, and its story began about a decade after the first trains ran in North America.

Crew members of New York, Ontario & Western train 32 pose next to their caboose around 1890. Four-wheel "bobbers" were common through the 1800s. This one still uses link-and-pin couplers (note the slot centered at the bottom of the end sill). The lenses built into the end of the car are illuminated by lanterns from the inside. *Robert F. Harding collection*

Railroads began connecting America's cities and towns in the 1830s. Although scheduled passenger service began immediately upon the completion of most lines between cities and local communities, the vast majority of trains were "mixed," consisting of both freight and passenger equipment. Most train crews consisted of an engineer, fireman, conductor, and one or more brakemen. Trains, however, did not yet have cabooses—their eventual development into rolling offices, observation platforms, and homes-away-from-home came about with the evolution of freight-only trains, longer trains and routes, and a great deal of chance and happenstance.

Conductors and brakemen

Since the earliest days the conductor has been in charge of the train. Folklore has it that in 1840 on the Erie Railroad, engineer Abraham Hammil and conductor Henry Ayres came to blows over who was boss. The conductor won, likely due to his reported 300-pound weight! Although the fight most likely did occur, precedent had long been set with the 1835 opening of the Boston & Providence Railroad. Its original rule book states: "The Conductor has sole charge of the train, he will tell the Engineman when to STOP and when to START." Regardless of origin, the conductor has always been responsible for the safety of his men, equipment, and passengers, and has been in charge of the paperwork associated with his train—be it waybills or passenger tickets—ever since.

Early trains (into the 1870s) lacked both air brakes and knuckle (Janney) couplers. Cars used link-and-pin couplers: An oval iron link was held by a pin on each car, and the links had to be guided into place by (and pins inserted by) a brakeman. This was extremely hazardous, and resulted in frequent injuries and deaths. A senior brakeman who still had all 10 fingers was rare.

Applying a train's brakes was likewise a

Brand-new Chicago, Milwaukee & St. Paul four-wheel caboose no. 0478 has just emerged from the railroad's West Milwaukee shops in the 1890s. It has a full cupola with marker lamps mounted atop it, and an equipment box below the frame. It has knuckle couplers, but not air brakes. It's 21'-8" long over the platforms and 15'-10" tall to the top of the marker.
TRAINS magazine collection

dangerous activity. Brakes on each car were manual, controlled by a wheel mounted on a vertical staff that extended above one end of each car. Brakes were applied and released by one or more "brakies" running along the car tops tightening or releasing each car's individual brake wheel, responding to whistle signals from the engineer. This was hazardous enough in daylight in good weather, much less in bad weather, night, or winter.

Although the conductor and brakemen could easily be seated in a three- or four-car

So many cabooses, so many names

What did railroads and crewmen call their cabooses? "Crummy," literally and figuratively, was a good bet and a common nickname, but it really depended on the locale and the road. In New England, the New Haven informally used "hack," while the Boston & Maine called them "buggies." Northern neighbors Canadian Pacific, Canadian National and Central Vermont all used the term "van." Ditto for the Southern Railway and Southern Pacific. The Pennsylvania Railroad preferred "cabins" or "cabin cars," while Conrail inherited both "vans" and "cabins." Midwestern roads Chicago, Burlington & Quincy and Chicago & North Western called them "waycars," as did Western road Santa Fe. Neighbor Illinois Central stuck with "caboose."

Nationwide, unofficial names included chariot, hack, parlor (or parlor car), and in reference—but not deference—to the conductor, brain box, monkey cage, and clown wagon. Likely the most poignant was "glory wagon," in homage to the hundreds of fellow crewmen killed in rear end collisions. Even the cupola had its own nicknames: "crow's nest" and "lookout" being most common. Like the word caboose, they too shared a nautical heritage.

A Virginian conductor and brakemen pose with their wood caboose around 1900. Note the chalk road name and number (complete with backward "N"). The two-truck caboose has air brakes and knuckle couplers. The broom tucked in the end grab iron appears to get heavy use. *H. Reid collection*

Freshly outshopped Milwaukee Road no. 0638, built around 1900, has the hallmarks of modern caboose design: a long body with end platforms, cupola (albeit with early built-in marker lamp on top), and a pair of four-wheel archbar trucks. *TRAINS magazine collection*

passenger train, freight trains of more than a dozen cars presented a major problem, since immediate braking was impossible—it could take several minutes for a brakeman to reach the rear of the train. With hills and curves (or at night), crew members aboard the engine could no longer easily see the rear end of the train for any potential problems there. The engine cab or deck was also crowded with additional crew members beyond the engineer and fireman, and the cab of a steam locomotive was not a good place to do paperwork.

Legend has it that conductor Nat Williams of the 26-mile Auburn & Syracuse (New York) Railroad had a better idea in the early 1840s. He had an empty boxcar added to the end of his local freight to serve as a

rolling office, complete with a barrel turned on end for a desk and a small wooden box for a chair. Suddenly, he not only had a place for his paperwork, but for lunch and dinner as well. The rest of the boxcar soon filled with lanterns, flags, and parts and tools of all kinds. Nat's idea outlasted his employer, as the A&S soon disappeared into the expanding New York Central System. As a logical solution to his workspace problem, Williams had incidentally fathered the conductor's car/caboose.

The pre-Civil War years found similar "conductor's cars" growing in popularity on America's expanding railroads. The conductor could process his waybills in comparative quiet—as compared to a steam locomotive cab—and the brakeman could watch the rear of the train from side doors. When it was necessary to apply the brakes, brakemen could now start at both ends of the train for quicker response time. It wasn't air brakes, but it was a great improvement!

Since cabooses were built of wood, like all 19th century railroad equipment, modifying them was all in a day's work for the car shop crew. In the early years an older wooden flatcar or boxcar was the usual starting point for building a home-grown caboose. These cars soon became the freight train's accepted—and official—end, be it a local or long-distance train.

By the time of the Civil War, the conductor's car had become universal, as had its name: *caboose*. No definitive history of the word "caboose" exists. However, Webster's Dictionary indicates the word is likely derived from the Dutch word *kabuis* or a similar German one, *kabuus*, both meaning "little room." In the 18th century the term referred to the galley—or small kitchen—on sailing ships. Since New York City was once the Dutch Colony of Nieuw (New) Amsterdam, and Dutch names still remain common in the Hudson River Valley, it seems logical that kabuis/kabuus was Americanized into "caboose." With descendants of Dutch settlers in the employ of the New York Central, Erie, Lackawanna, and/or the other numerous railroads in eastern New York and New Jersey, "caboose" gradually entered common usage.

Cupolas and platforms

By the 1860s the little flat-roofed caboose was due for its next—and most recognizable—improvement, the cupola. A specific man and railroad is recorded for inventing the cupola. It was on the Chicago & North Western, and the intrepid conductor was T. B. Watson. Rolling across Iowa in a company-built caboose one night in 1863, Watson noted that the flat roof had a hole in it large enough for a man's shoulders to pass through. Curious, he found something (presumably a couple of wooden boxes) to stand or sit on—and stuck his head out. Enthralled, he remained there throughout the remainder of the trip. He promptly bullied or cajoled the shop superintendent into building an observation deck, or cupola, on the caboose. Thanks to his chance experience, cupolas would remain

Caboose interiors varied widely in design, but through the steam era included the same basic elements. This staged photo shows a crewman (left) about to climb the cupola steps while three others gather at the conductor's desk. The stove at left, with ever-present coffee pot or kettle, was a staple of caboose life. *Canadian National*

A primary purpose of the caboose was serving as the conductor's office. A desk with multiple slots and cubbyholes and a kerosene lantern firmly attached to the wall complete this 1940s scene. *W.A. Akin*

next edition, in 1884, stated "cabooses are often made with lookouts for displaying train signals to locomotives and following trains, and to give trainmen a view of the train."

While the cupola was slowly growing in popularity, another modification improved Nat Williams' humble wooden boxcar. The side doors for crew access were replaced by end platforms with attached steps. These platforms gave crew members direct access to the car(s) ahead of them, including ladders for reasonably safe access to the roofs and car tops as well. The rear platform was a wonderful place on long curves to lean out and check the train for anything amiss, or to inspect a passing train rolling by on a neighboring track and give a wave or highball signal to a passing train, tower operator, station agent, or yard crew. The steps made it much easier and safer to board and dismount the car, and a trainman could easily stand on the caboose's rear platform steps to snag train orders on the fly from a station agent.

Through the last two decades of the 19th century, U.S. railroads gradually developed a

a caboose hallmark for a century and a quarter.

Although cupolas would eventually become standard on cabooses, it would take a couple of decades. In his 1968 book *The Railroad Caboose,* author William F. Knapke notes that the first edition of the *Master Car Builder's Dictionary* in 1874 discusses cabooses but doesn't mention cupolas; however, the

"We got us a Burlington man here"

We rolled to a stop on the outskirts of Cass Lake, Minn., long past midnight that frigid night back in March 1982. I was riding Burlington Northern train 127 west out of Superior, Wis., as part of a plan to track down the last of BN's Twin Cities Region-based F units before they became extinct. I leaned against the control stand in the lead SD40-2 and listened as first Fred Levin, our engineer, then Ted Kivi, our conductor in the caboose on the rear of the train, called the BN Cass Lake operator on the radio. Finally, after failing to raise either him, the Grand Rapids operator, or the BN 5th Subdivision dispatcher 160 miles east in Superior, Levin and Kivi decided to cut the motive power off the train and run engine-light (without cars in tow, that is) into town.

The head-end members of the Grand Forks (N.Dak.) relief crew that had been called to take our train west, back to their home terminal, stood outside on the depot platform and stared up at us as if we were the Four Horsemen of the Apoc-

alypse. Inside the Cass Lake depot, the third-trick operator explained that he'd been talking with a Soo Line train an hour or so before we had tip-toed into town, and he'd forgotten to turn the radio back to the BN road channel. It made sense once Levin explained to me that Soo had trackage rights over BN between Soo Junction at MP 155.4 and Bemidji, Minn., 15 miles west of Cass Lake.

A few minutes later, the new engineer and head-end brakeman climbed aboard the power and took it back to the outskirts of town to retrieve the 140 cars of our train. After a time, 127 materialized out of the darkness and clomped past the platform kicking up a swirl of snow. After Kivi and his rear-end brakey bailed off the rolling caboose and landed on the platform, the Grand Forks rear-end men swung aboard, and the last I saw of train 127 was a glimmer of yellow light from the inside of its caboose fading into the night.

It wasn't until Levin, Kivi, the rest of the crew, and I were on

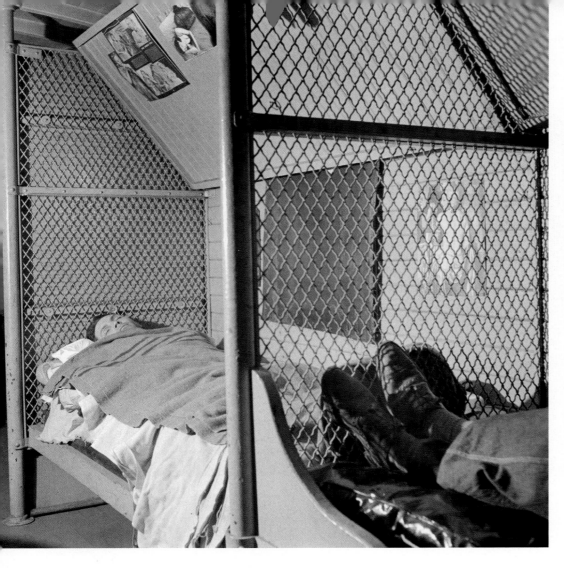

Crew members often slept aboard their cabooses while away from home terminals. The upper berth is folded up and not in use. This caboose is stopped; men sleeping while trains were in motion slept with feet toward the locomotive in case of slack running in. This is on the Santa Fe in California.
Jack Delano; Library of Congress

our way up to the motel where BN's crews laid over that I realized I'd forgotten to write down the number of 127's caboose. I pulled out my pen and notebook, leaned over the front seat of the four-door sedan that served as a taxicab, and asked Kivi if he remembered the number of our waycar.

For a moment there was dead silence. Then Kivi said, "The what?"

"The number," I said, flipping open my notebook to a blank page. Then, thinking he hadn't heard me the first time, I added, "Of the waycar."

"Christ," Kivi groaned, "We got us a damn Burlington man here!"

I smiled uncertainly as Kivi twisted around in the front seat and said to Levin, "Hey, Fred, you have any waycars on the old NP?"

"Nope," said Levin, shaking his head. "We had cabooses."

"Yeah, that's what we used on the Great Northern, cabooses. I don't know what the hell a waycar is. Something you weigh cars with, I guess."

Egad, I thought, now I've stepped in it. Never mind that I'd actually hired out on the BN in 1976, six years after the Chicago, Burlington & Quincy had been folded into BN's camp; obviously the last six or eight months I'd spent working the second trick HY operator's job at BN's former CB&Q yard in Cicero had had an impact on my vocabulary. I didn't dare tell them that where I'd been hanging around on BN's Chicago Region (which was all former CB&Q territory), they called dwarf signals pots, locomotives motors, and Burlington's freight F units graybacks. Well, I thought, it proved something. Even after 12 years of a sometimes contentious merger on the BN, you could at least get an NP and a GN person to agree on one thing: the Burlington people were weird. And they proved it by what they called their cabooses.— *Paul Schneider*

Missouri Pacific conductor Glenn Voyles is on the radio telephone talking to the head end while holding onto the "monkey bar" of his modern bay window caboose in 1977. Air pressure gauge and brake valve are to the right; the oil stove is behind Voyles at left. *Wayne Leeman*

A brakeman prepares dinner aboard an Indiana Harbor Belt caboose between Chicago and Hammond, Ind., in January 1943. Crews often made meals using nothing more than a skillet, saucepan, and the caboose stove; crew members who could cook well were highly valued. *Jack Delano, Library of Congress*

The Pennsylvania Railroad was among the first lines to add radio communication to cabooses with its TrainPhone (induction-type) system in the 1940s (note the loudspeaker in the cupola). Note also the long bench-style seat in the cupola above the lockers, instead of chair-style seats.
Pennsylvania RR

The crew of a Chicago Great Western caboose gives a friendly wave to bystanders around 1950. The steel caboose is one of 25 built in 1945-1946 by Pullman-Standard.
Basil W. Koob

A public connection

The caboose cupola not only advanced the safety and productivity of train crews but also gave a curious public a better look at the men who had signed on for railroading's great adventure. Engineers and small-town telegraphers probably enjoyed greater status as heroes to small boys, but a wave from the rocking red ark at the end of a train was to become a happily anticipated element of trackside life for males and females of all ages in every post-Civil War generation. "It has an upstairs and a downstairs, a front porch and a back porch," went one woman's succinct analysis of the caboose's architectural and social charms. "And it's cute."

In its busiest hour, the caboose was a daily sight on railroads throughout North America, bringing up the rear of mainline manifests and local freights, riding the spindly wooden trestles of the Colorado narrow gauges, serving as primary elements of mixed trains on short lines and branches of major systems, and shepherding the freight of a surprising number of interurban lines. Wherever freight-carrying rails and human activity crossed paths, it was a rare day which did not see at least one encounter between man and caboose.

To plowing farmers, commuting workers, or any of life's multitudinous varieties of sidewalk superintendents, the rear-end trainman's friendly acknowledgment of momentarily intersecting lives, careers, and fortunes added a melodic note to otherwise mundane workdays, a signal of accomplishment as pronounced as the arrival of the newspaper on the front porch or the blast of the plant whistle at 5 o'clock. As a part of the fabric of one's hometown, the caboose easily outranked innumerable politicians and sweethearts in popularity and longevity. And, in the era of billboard boxcars when Westerners speculated as to whether Phoebe Snow was a gentrywoman on the order of Alice Roosevelt Longworth and Easterners wondered how a railroad that ended in Colorado and Wyoming could correctly claim to go "Everywhere West," the caboose provided a brief paragraph of summation to the multi-messaged travelogue of a passing freight. The coming of the automobile age only heightened public anticipation of the caboose's arrival; for idled grade-crossing grammarians it offered an exuberant exclamation point at the end of a fast-stepping time freight, or the long-awaited period of a plodding coal drag.—*William Benning Stewart, from "The End,"* Trains *magazine, August 1990*

series of uniform industry standards for all types of equipment, particularly rolling stock. Union agreements, railroad safety rules, and individual state laws regarding crew size and safety provided guidelines for requirements for caboose construction and equipment (interior and exterior). Within those height, width, buff/draft strength, and other limits, the caboose-building industry grew.

Cabooses were built in a variety of styles, sizes, and designs by railroads' own shops as well as the dozens of car builders of the period. Wood construction was universal into the early 1900s, with vertical tongue-and-groove sheathing standard (as with freight cars such as boxcars and refrigerator cars).

Many early small cabooses (bodies around 17 feet long and coupled length of 21 feet) rode on four wheels instead of conventional trucks. These cabooses, often called "bobbers," were common on Northeastern railroads and could also be found on other railroads across the country. They were economical to build

Michigan Central no. 1837 is an all-wood caboose built in 1911. Sliding-style windows with mullions were common on early wood cars. The car rides on passenger-style wood-beam trucks, known for providing an extremely smooth ride.
Library of Congress

Number of cabooses in service

1880: 5,500
1900: 17,600
1925: 34,000
1950: 25,000
1980: 13,000
1998: 3,000

and worked well at slow speeds, but did not track well at higher speeds and proved to be unstable in collisions and derailments, often tipping over. Many were removed from service by the 1900s, although some remained on local and transfer runs into the 1940s (and some new ones were built into the 1920s).

Longer cabooses riding on pairs of four-wheel trucks were the norm by the late 1890s, especially in the West where clearances weren't as tight. Long cabooses were more stable and rode better, and they provided ample room inside for all of the equipment and supplies that had become required for operations.

Interiors

Specific interior equipment varied in style, arrangement, and design by railroad, but the basic list of furnishings and supplies (required by union agreements and various laws) remained relatively constant among all cabooses. Through the end of the steam era (and into the 1960s in many areas), cabooses were assigned to individual conductors, and the caboose served as the home away from home for the conductor and other trainmen—cabooses often served as sleeping

quarters and a rolling home that crewmen shared during the layover at their "away" terminal. This meant interior furnishings were a combination of work-related equipment and various living and comfort amenities.

During the era of assigned cabooses, cabooses were switched on and off trains at division and subdivision points whenever trains changed crews. Crews took great pride in their cars: Interiors of assigned cars were often decorated with curtains, calendars, artwork (pinups were common), and other personal touches, and most of these cars were scrupulously clean.

The caboose served as the conductor's office, so it included a desk for his paperwork, an accompanying chair, and cubbyholes and drawers for paper forms, timetables, waybills, and other materials. To enable the conductor and others to see their work at night, an ingenious mounting arrangement was created for the kerosene lantern. Its base went in a wall-mounted bracket, while farther up on the bracket the lantern's glass chimney was held securely by a coiled steel "doughnut" which slid down over it.

Canadian Pacific's standard wood caboose design, with its distinctive tall cupola, dates to 1905. Versions built after 1912, such as no. 436355, were built on steel center sills. This one is at Brownsville Junction, Maine. *J.D. Bennett*

The Pennsylvania was the first railroad to build steel cabooses on a large scale with its N5 class, starting in 1914. Number 477027, built in 1916, wears a War Bonds slogan in this 1944 view. The 2A-F5 trucks were common on PRR steel cabooses. *Pennsylvania RR*

Bunks were provided, with various arrangements. Typical was a pair of permanent low-level bunks (running lengthwise with the car) with a fold-down upper bunk above each. The upper was folded up when not in use, providing seating during the daytime on the lower.

A stove was necessary equipment, bolted firmly in place with a vertical pipe leading to a smoke jack on the roof. The stoves provided heat for the car in cold weather and their flat tops served as a cooking stove for meals. Through the steam era it was common for the whole crew to chip in for the groceries, with meals cooked on the stove. Of course, a good cook was an asset to any crew.

Coal stoves were typical through the steam era, with a small coal bunker built

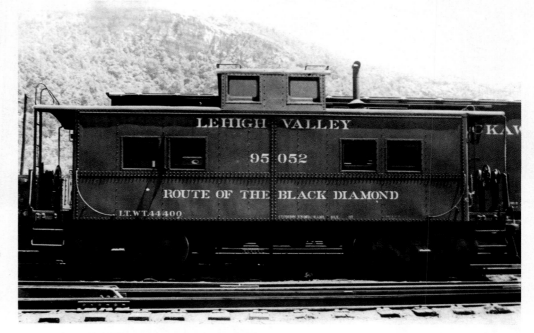

into the end of the car. By the 1950s, fuel-oil heaters replaced coal stoves, with an external filler pipe usually visible on the outside of the car.

Storage lockers and cabinets held a variety of supplies, including tools, cooking utensils and food, crew members' grips (suitcases) and jackets, journal-box oil (and cotton waste for packing), lanterns (and fuel), and spare coupler knuckles. A rerailing frog, chains, jack, and blocks were also common.

Water was provided for both drinking and washing (usually in separate tanks, each labeled), with a neighboring wash basin. Toilets, however, didn't become common until the 1940s and later, when they became required by union agreements.

On the end wall next to the door you'll find racks for fusees (flares used for signaling), torpedoes (small explosive packs that can be strapped to a rail to signal or warn a train), flags (for markers and for manually signaling following trains), chalk (for marking sides of freight cars), and a first-aid kit.

Built-in steps in the middle of the car led to elevated seats in the cupola. These seats were generally built above storage lockers and cabinets. Most common was a seat on each end of each side; some cabooses had a

single bench, meaning a crew member had to sit with his legs straight out as if on a couch. Modern cabooses typically had "walkover" seats: A seat in the middle with a back that could be moved over the seat, allowing the brakeman or conductor to sit facing either direction.

By the early 1900s, cabooses were equipped with a long grab iron running the length of the interior near the ceiling. This provided a safety rail to hold onto while standing or moving, protecting crews from slack action that could easily knock a person over and cause injury.

A critical interior component was the air brake pressure gauge and valve, located on a wall on or near the cupola. The gauge registered the air pressure in the train line at the caboose—critical information for safe operation—and the valve allowed opening the train line to "dump the air"—letting the air escape to apply the emergency brakes if necessary.

Some cabooses were equipped with air whistles (sometimes called "peanut whistles"), powered by the train line and controlled by a valve by the conductor. These were used during reverse moves across grade crossings and, in pre-radio days, for communicating signals to the head end.

The Chicago, Burlington & Quincy was among railroads adopting sleek, streamlined designs for steel cabooses in the 1950s. The Q's class NE-12 cars, built in 1954, had tall, angled cupolas and debuted the silver paint scheme with red and black striping. It was the start of the "little red caboose" getting bright and colorful new paint schemes. Number 13572 is at Eola, Ill., in 1960. *Henry E. Bender Jr.*

Markers make a train a train

A steel caboose carries the markers on an Erie freight train passing west of Suffern, N.Y., on October 26, 1947. The kerosene lanterns, hung on brackets at each rear corner, signify the official end of the train.
Ollie Fife

As iconic as cabooses were, they did not by themselves constitute the end of a train (nor were they even, in fact, part of the definition of a train). Railroad rules define a train as "an engine, with or without cars, displaying a marker."

You'll notice that the definition of "train" contains no mention of cabooses, observation cars, drumhead signs, or end-of-train (EOT) devices. Markers are what let railroad personnel (crews on other trains, station operators, tower operators, work gangs, etc.) know when a train is actually a train and—importantly—when that train has officially passed a location. A switch engine pulling 125 cars in a yard isn't a train—unless it carries a marker on the last car. A train has not passed a station, another train, or other location until the markers have passed. Then and only then

can an operator "OS" a train (report it to the dispatcher and mark it "on sheet").

What constitutes a "marker" has changed over the years, and individual railroads have specified their requirements in their rulebooks as useage has evolved. In the early days of railroading, a simple red flag by day and a red lantern by night usually served as a marker. From the late 1800s through the steam era, cabooses, passenger cars, and the rears of locomotive tenders (but not freight cars) were fitted with brackets for mounting a pair of specially designed kerosene lanterns. These four-sided lanterns generally had a red lens on one side and green lenses on the other three. When running, the red lens was displayed to the rear of the train with green lenses to the sides and front; when a train pulled in the clear at a passing siding, a crewman

turned the markers to show green to the rear. (Some railroads, including the Santa Fe, specified yellow lights instead of green.) Specific indications could vary based on double-track operation or other situations (see the excerpts from the CB&Q rulebook at right). In daytime, green flags were used as a marker (although the rule allowed for a red flag to be used if the last car was a car not equipped to carry markers—a red flag placed in the coupler of the trailing boxcar, for example).

In the late 1950s and 1960s the display of markers was simplified as cabooses were being equipped with electric lights. On some roads, reflectorized paddles carried in the old lamp brackets replaced traditional lamps. Another approach was to equip cabooses with one or two built-in red and green marker lights at each end, or on the roof as on Southern Pacific bay-window cars. Passenger trains could use a single red light hung on the tail gate of the last car.

Today's EOT devices have marker lights (now typically flashing LEDs) built in. Many railroads now allow the trailing headlight, set on dim, to serve as a marker when an engine is running light or serving as a rear pusher locomotive; other locomotives have a red light near the headlight for this purpose.

Markers have changed considerably over 160 years of railroading, but their purpose remains the same: Railroaders know a train is intact when they see its marker.
—Harry J. Dolan, retired Norfolk Southern trainmaster

From the Chicago, Burlington & Quincy 1951 *Rules of the Operating Department:*

Rule S-19: The following signals will be displayed to the rear of every train, as markers, to indicate the rear of the train:

(a). By day, marker lamps not lighted, or green flags, in places provided.

(b). By night, marker lamps lighted, displaying red to the rear:

(1). On single track;

(2). With the current of traffic on two tracks;

(3). On two or more tracks, where trains are governed by signal indication.

(c). By night, marker lamps lighted, displaying green to the rear on the side next to the main track on which current of traffic is moving and red to the rear on the opposite side.

(1). When running against the current of traffic on train order authority or when standing against the current of traffic;

(2). When using a branch main track or a long lead that parallels the main track.

(d). When a train is clear of the main track to be passed by a following train, lighted marker lamps must be changed to display green to the rear, but before main track is again fouled must be restored to display red to the rear.

(g). Unless otherwise provided, markers must not be removed until the train has been delivered to connecting crew or is clear of the main track and the switch is closed.

Santa Fe brakeman Kenneth N. Dean hangs a marker on his caboose in March 1943. *Jack Delano; Library of Congress*

Red flags serve as markers on this Burlington Northern wide-cupola caboose along the Mississippi River in August 1976. The caboose, built by International, also has permanent electric marker lights added under the center of the roof overhang. *Russ Porter; Don Heimburger collection*

International's wide-cupola cabooses represented the ultimate in modern design. Northern Pacific 10401, built in 1969, was among the last built with rooftop running boards. It has permanently mounted electric markers at each corner, and it rides on roller-bearing caboose trucks.
International Car Co.

As cabooses evolved, so did their interiors. Radios began appearing in the 1940s and became common by the following decade. Radio handsets (which looked like conventional telephone handsets) were mounted so crewman had easy access from both the cupola or bay window and the conductor's desk. With radios came electric power, with generators (powered by axle-mounted pulleys) charging batteries to power internal lights, markers as well as radio.

Furnishings became more spartan with the move toward pool cabooses by the 1960s. Improved oil stoves and heaters replaced coal, with additional safety railings. Desks and furnishings had rounded corners and padding for safety. Bunks became less common (or fewer in number) as it became more common for crews to stay in motels or other off-line housing while on the road. Retention toilets became mandatory equipment.

Steel frames and bodies

By the turn of the 20th century, thanks to the advent of knuckle couplers, automatic air brakes, and improved (and larger) locomotives, freight trains were growing longer, heavier, and faster. Unfortunately, this meant railroad accidents were also becoming more severe, and rear-end collisions were all too common.

By the 1910s, the solution to this was steel center sills and full steel underframes on wood cars. Many older wood cars were eventually built with steel frames; new cars typically had wood bodies with steel framing atop steel underframes. By World War I, when the United States Railroad Administration took over the nation's railroads (from 1917 to 1920), all-steel freight cars were becoming more common, with steel underframes on most cars. By the 1920s and 1930s, steel construction was extended to cabooses as well, greatly improving crew safety. Continuing public and regulatory concerns about crew safety were a big reason for the change to all-steel construction; steel cars also required less maintenance and lasted longer. The era of new wood cabooses had passed, although many older wood cabooses survived many decades in service—some lasting into the 1970s (albeit with substantial rebuilding).

An additional benefit of the steel-underframe and all-steel caboose was that it could withstand the buff forces when a large modern steam engine (such as a 4-8-4 or a 4-6-6-4) or a multi-unit diesel in helper or pusher service coupled up and placed 100,000 or more pounds of tractive force against the rear coupler. Steel cabooses eliminated the extra switching movements required to place a wooden caboose behind the pusher (more on that in Chapter 7).

Although the shift from wood to more durable steel construction began in the 1910s, caboose technology itself didn't change much initially. Bigger changes followed World War I as smoother-riding

swing-motion caboose trucks and early cushion underframes (such as the Duryea) were introduced in the 1920s.

Specific crew requirements and external and interior equipment and facilities of most cabooses were subject to a combination of legal requirements (many state laws were very specific about equipment required) and local union agreements that varied from railroad to railroad, state to state, and even divisions on one railroad. Height and width clearances could also vary among divisions and railroads. All of this meant that each caboose had to have the right equipment and comply with clearance restrictions or it couldn't be used on a specific subdivision, route, or train.

The Pennsylvania Railroad, in keeping with its self-proclaimed status as "The Standard Railroad of the World" was the first to begin building a fleet of new steel cabooses (which it called "cabin cars") with its class N5 cars in 1914. These would indeed become a standard, and readily identifiable by their centered (angled-side) cupolas, steel roof that wrapped around the tops of the

Some railroads rebuilt old cabooses into yard or transfer cabooses, removing the cupola and remodeling the interior. Great Northern wood car X607 is stenciled for yard service only at Seattle in October 1954.
Bob's Photo;
Don Heimburger collection

Cabooses with side doors were often used on branch and secondary lines for delivering express and less-than-carload (LCL) packages, crates, and parcels. This Cotton Belt crew poses with their wooden side-door car in 1910.
W.T. Church collection

sides, and rectangular windows at the end of each side. Distinctive follow-ups were the N5c cars of 1942, which had pairs of round porthole windows at the end of each side; and larger N8 cars of 1950.

Another common early steel car was the so-called "Northeastern" caboose, designed and first built by the Reading in 1924 and soon common on railroads throughout the region (and, through resales, eventually across the country). These had centered cupolas with eight windows and a distinctive body window pattern (four on each side; two toward each end). See Chapter 4 for details and examples.

Many other railroads acquired significant fleets of new steel cars in distinctive styles and designs, notably the Santa Fe with its end-cupola cars built starting in 1927 (rebuilt as CE-1 and later designations starting in 1966); and the Union Pacific with

its tall-cupola CA-3 and following designs beginning in 1942.

Streamlined designs became popular after World War II. Among the best-known were the Wabash and Burlington angled-cupola designs: the Wabash C-18 class, built starting in 1945 (which later went to Ann Arbor and to Norfolk & Western), and the CB&Q with its NE-12 of 1954 (many of which survived to Burlington Northern).

Bay windows and wide cupolas

The idea had been tried in the 1920s, but in the late 1930s the Milwaukee Road and Baltimore & Ohio built the first "modern" versions of the bay window designs, with a section of each side wall extended outward 12 to 18 inches. Both experimented with designs that resulted in distinctive cars: The Milwaukee's of 1939 featured all-welded construction with distinctive horizontal ribs;

the B&O's (the first 100 production cars were built in 1941) featured the same "wagon-top" design as many of its new freight cars, with the roof wrapping down to the sides in a continuous piece, with vertical stabilizing posts that continue across the roof.

Seated at the desk in the bay window, the conductor could now view the side of his train without climbing into the cupola or out onto the rear platform. The safety hazards (climbing a ladder and sitting on an elevated seat of a moving train) and the structural requirements integral to the cupola (as well as vertical clearance issues) were eliminated in the bay-window design.

After World War II, bay window cabooses became very popular among many railroads across the country. Some railroads built their own, starting with older wood or steel-body cabooses, removing the cupola, and adding bays. Others built them new or bought them from manufacturers such as International Car Co., which became a popular builder of new steel cabooses starting in the 1950s.

The Milwaukee Road built several transfer cabooses atop old tender frames in the mid-1950s. Number 990035, here in 1974, was built as no. 01734 in 1956. It has a 12-foot body on a 32-foot frame; a couple of porch chairs provide seating on the end. *Don Heimburger collection*

Lake Superior & Ishpeming side-door caboose no. 9 pauses at Marquette, Mich., in September 1962. Many railroads continued using wood side-door cars in local freight service into the 1960s. *Henry E. Bender; Don Heimburger collection*

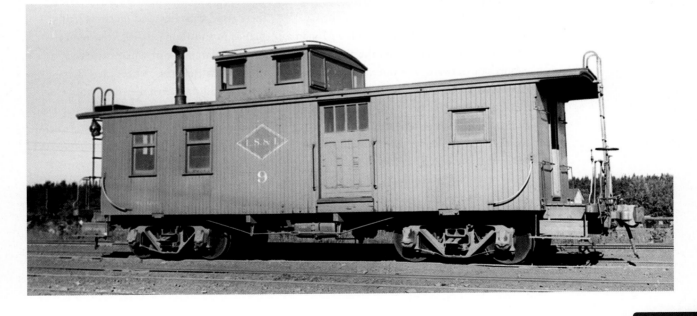

The bay window design had been used since the 1920s, but the Milwaukee Road and Baltimore & Ohio were the first to develop successful steel designs. Milwaukee Road's welded cars, built starting in 1939, had distinctive horizontal ribs, or stiffeners. They rode on passenger-style trucks. *Don Heimburger collection*

Major railroads operating large numbers of steel bay window cabooses included Chicago & North Western; New York Central; Southern Ry.; Southern Pacific; and Western Pacific.

The bay-window concept was eventually modified to include the cupola. The Chicago Great Western and Monon experimented with extending the cupola outward from the body to provide a better view of the train: the CGW on older wood cars it rebuilt, and the Monon with Thrall, by extending just the above-roof cupola side outward. The International Car Co. began building commercial versions in 1952, delivering the first to Duluth, Missabe & Iron Range. These have the body of the cupola extending out past the car side and below the roof line. They have been called wide-cupola, wide-vision, and extended-vision cabooses, and regardless of name they quickly became popular, especially with Midwestern and Western roads. International continued building them for dozens of railroads into the 1970s; other builders turned them out as well (see Chapter 5).

Transfers, combines, and drover cars

Cabooses are not a one-size-fits-all proposition. Much like boxcars have many variations to haul different products, cabooses came in many sizes and variations to perform specific jobs.

Among the most common—and still in use in some areas—were transfer cabooses. These were typically used on short hauls, such as in shuttling cars between major yards in a large city or when switching urban industrial areas, where crew living quarters and train visibility were not required (no cupola or bay window needed). Interior details are generally spartan: a desk and chair or chairs, a stove, and safety/flagging equipment, but no bunks, cupola, or bay window, and fewer storage lockers and cabinets. The car basically serves as a platform and shelter for crew members.

Railroads sometimes built their own transfer cabooses from older road cabooses by removing the cupola and stripping down the interior. New transfer cabooses typically ride on flatcar-type frames, leaving large porches on each end.

Cabooses on branchline trains through the steam and early diesel eras often provided additional services, with crews delivering express and/or less-than-carload (LCL) shipments and parcels (this was done with express/baggage cars or boxcars on main lines and heavy-traffic lines). Many of these branchline trains were also required by law to provide passenger service, which was done for (usually) infrequent riders by providing a seat in the caboose.

For these services, many railroads operated cabooses with side doors and interior storage areas for boxes and parcels. Some included limited bench seating for passengers. Known as combine cabooses, branchline cabooses, or side-door cabooses, some resembled standard cabooses with added doors; others were much longer (stretching to 50 feet or more) with additional side windows marking the location of the passenger seats. Most were retired in the 1950s and '60s as railroads left the express and LCL business and were allowed to abandon branchline passenger service (and often the lines themselves).

Other cars resembled cabooses or were rebuilt from older cabooses for other service. Among the most common were drover cars, used as bunk and traveling cars by cowboys accompanying cars of cattle to market. Other variations include bunk cars, business cars, and test cars of varying styles.

Demise

As distinctive as cabooses were, and as much of an icon as they were to railroading, there was no escaping their largest shortcoming: They were extremely expensive. Not only were cabooses expensive to purchase (especially the more technologically advanced versions of the 1960s and later), they cost a great deal to maintain and operate. As train crew sizes were reduced through the 1960s and 1970s, the need for cabooses began

International Car Co. became a prominent builder of standard-design bay window cabooses beginning in the 1950s. Rock Island 17072 was built by ICC in 1966 and actually owned by Union Pacific, which leased this group of cars to the Rock. Note the roof-mounted electric markers (above the bay).
Don Heimburger collection

Drovers' cars provided riding space for ranch hands accompanying livestock to market. They often resembled cabooses. Chicago & North Western no. 10802 was built by AC&F in 1909; it was restored at Mid-Continent Railway Museum in North Freedom, Wis., where it is shown in 1997.
Don Heimburger

dropping. From a peak of 34,000 cabooses in service in the late 1920s, the number in service dropped to 15,000 by the late 1960s and 12,000 by 1984.

Thanks to technology and a 1982 agreement between railroads and the United Transportation Union, the caboose began disappearing rapidly from mainline use between 1982 and the mid-1990s. The first to go were those on long-distance trains, unit trains, and other non-stop runs that did no en-route switching. Cabooses continued to be used in local freight and transfer service, and in some states that required cabooses by law, but by 1990 most cabooses had been replaced by a small box called an end-of-train device, or EOT or ETD (also known as a FRED, short for "flashing rear-end device," in early days). The EOT's flashing red light serves as a rear marker, and the device monitors train line pressure and constantly communicates via radio signal with a monitor on the locomotive. Modern versions allow two-way communication and controls. EOTs are compact, mount in or on the rear coupler of the train's last car, and save railroads millions of dollars annually on crew, equipment and

maintenance costs.

However, no matter how technically sophisticated EOTs become, they will never attain the rank that the Little Red Caboose has in our cultural and railroad heritage. A crewman's friendly wave from the cupola or rear platform was a national institution for more than 150 years. Once taken for granted, it now is all but gone. Railroads' balance sheets are better with EOTs, but the railroad industry's public image has faded perceptibly with the caboose's removal.

Today, only a few short lines and some local/transfer freights around major cities still use cabooses, mainly serving as a platform for a rear-end crew needed for the large amount of switching or reverse moves over public grade crossings that need to be done. Few have cupolas or bay windows, and they no longer serve as the offices on wheels that they once were. Hundreds remain scattered across North America, reborn into cabins, offices, hotel rooms, business establishments of all types, and any other use an individual can find for them. Even *The Little Red Caboose* is still in print, nearly 70 years after its initial publication.

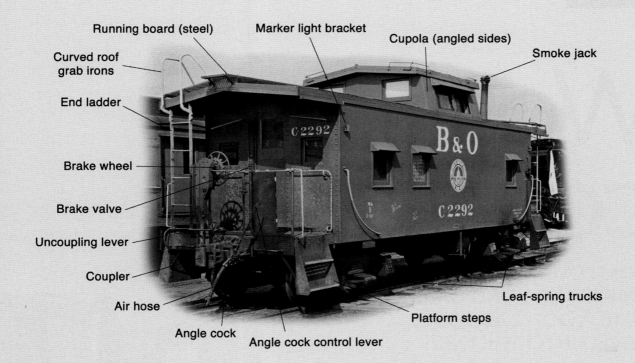

Running board (steel) · Marker light bracket · Cupola (angled sides) · Smoke jack · Curved roof grab irons · End ladder · Brake wheel · Brake valve · Uncoupling lever · Coupler · Air hose · Angle cock · Angle cock control lever · Platform steps · Leaf-spring trucks

B&O C2292

Spotting features

Here are some things to watch for in identifying specific caboose models and car series:

Size. Cabooses vary by body and frame length; width; wheelbase length; and height. Cabooses on Western railroads tend to be longer and taller; clearance restrictions in the Northeast mean cabooses there tend to be shorter and narrower.

Construction material. Is the body wood or steel? If the body is wood, is the underframe wood (visible truss rods) or steel? For steel: Are seams riveted or welded? What's the pattern of rivet lines, batten strips, or weld seams?

Style. Cabooses fall into three basic types: cupola, bay window, or transfer. For a cupola caboose: How large is the cupola? How tall is it compared to the body? Is the cupola centered or toward an end? Are the sides and/or ends angled inward? How many windows on the cupola? Is the cupola wider than the body? For bay window cabooses: Does the protruding bay extend the full height of the body or is it partial? What is the window pattern and how large are the windows on each side? For a transfer caboose: Does it follow traditional construction or does it have large end platforms?

Window location and style. How many windows are on each side and end? How large are they? Are they square, rectangular, rectangular with rounded corners, or round? Opening or non-opening? Sliding windows with mullions (similar to structure windows) were common on early cabooses. Sliding screens were also often used. By the 1960s, safety glass was

Baltimore & Ohio C2292 is a class I-5D car, identifiable by its longer wheelbase and narrower end platforms compared to an I-5. It has been rebuilt with plywood side sheathing, vertically mounted brake wheels, cast trucks, and an oil stove (note filler at far right of side). It's at Toledo, Ohio, in October 1962. *Jim Hediger*

required, and many window openings were plated over.

Trucks. Cabooses rode on a variety of trucks, which differed from standard freight-car trucks. Many used archbar trucks or other older designs much longer than freight cars. Leaf-spring designs (instead of coil springs) were most common.

Roofs. Is the roof wood, sheathed in tarpaper or metal sheets, or is it made from self-supporting steel panels? How does the roof terminate at the sides? Is it curved (radial) or peaked? Check the style and location of smoke jack, antennas, vents (for the toilet), air conditioners, and other details. Is the running board wood or steel, or has it been removed?

Platforms and railings: Check the shape and style of steps (cast or fabricated), platforms, railings, and ladders. Do ladder sides continue upward at the roof line, or are separate railings used (and what is their shape)? What type of brake wheel and brake valve are used?

Body details: Check for visible brake gear (K brakes on early cars, AB brakes after the 1930s), visible side sills (and whether ends of bolsters and cross bearers are visible), below-body tool and equipment boxes, and grab iron style and placement. Does the car have brackets for separate marker lanterns or built-in electric marker lamps? Does it have an axle-powered generator and a fuel filler for the stove?

Chapter 2

Wooden cabooses

**FROM FOUR-WHEEL
BOBBERS TO LONG CARS,
SOME WOOD CABOOSES
SERVED INTO THE 1980S**

ERIE

ERIE

04930

A classic Erie wood caboose pauses at Suffern, N.Y., in 1955. The Erie had a large fleet of wood cabooses built from the late 1910s through 1921. These featured three side windows with staggered spacing, radial (rounded) car and cupola roofs with roof sheathing wrapping over the top of the side, and a single centered side window on the cupola.
Claude K. Focht; Trains magazine collection

As with other freight cars through the 1890s, cabooses were built of wood, including framing, body sheathing, and underframes. The only major steel components were the trucks, couplers, and brake gear. Wood cars were relatively inexpensive to build and easy to repair and modify by railroad shop forces. Unfortunately, they also aged quickly and were too-easily damaged in accidents.

Their ease of construction meant many railroads built them in their own shops; hundreds of others were built by the dozens of car builders in business at the time (Central Locomotive & Car Works; Haskell & Barker; Laconia Car Co.; and American Car & Foundry among others). This

meant that early wood cars had distinctive appearances that varied greatly from builder to builder and railroad to railroad. Some were quite ornate, with fancy trimwork; others were plain and utilitarian.

By the 1880s, the adoption of knuckle couplers and air brakes was beginning to

Western railroads, which generally didn't face the severe clearance restrictions of Eastern lines, moved to larger (longer and taller) cabooses by the end of the 1800s. This Union Pacific caboose, at Grand Island, Neb., in 1898, has horizontal sheathing, tall sloped-side cupola with built-in marker compartment, six side windows, and distinctive ball-style markers. *Union Pacific*

A Cincinnati Northern (New York Central subsidiary) freight train crew poses with four-wheel caboose no. 98 somewhere in Ohio in 1915. The car has a tall cupola compared to other bobber cabooses. *TRAINS magazine collection*

Reading had more than 1,000 four-wheel cars in operation by 1900, including more than 400 class NMA cars. They had a pair of high-mounted side windows and rather conventional cupolas with two windows on each side. Number 90276 is one of several NMA cars that lasted in service into the late 1940s. *M.D. McCarter collection*

Pennsylvania built hundreds of four-wheel cabooses with steel underframes and wood bodies, class ND, starting in 1904. Most were rebuilt to eight-wheel cars in the 1910s, but some survived much longer. The crew of no. 476488, built in 1906, is gathered on the end platform in this late 1940s scene. *M.D. McCarter collection*

Among the last four-wheel cabooses built were a series of eight built by Pacific Electric at its Torrance (Calif.) shops in 1921. They lacked cupolas, had two side windows, and had a rudimentary sprung suspension between the axles. Many, including no. 1952, ran into the 1940s and '50s. *M.D. McCarter; Don Heimburger collection*

give cabooses a "modern" look. Bodies varied in length, but by that period most featured end platforms and cupolas. Cabooses of the time generally followed two basic designs: like conventional freight cars, supported on a pair of four-wheel trucks; or with shorter (20-foot or so) bodies atop just two axles (four total wheels). Four-wheel cabooses, nicknamed "bobbers," were lighter and less expensive to build, but didn't ride or track as well as conventional designs on two trucks.

Although two-truck designs would become standard in most areas by the late 1890s, plenty of four-wheel cabooses remained in operation (and a surprising number were still built after 1900); some would run into the 1940s and later.

Bobbers

Four-wheel cars date back to the first railroads. By the 1850s, the conductor's car was individually constructed for the specific purpose, and no longer merely a rebuilt boxcar. Because building cabooses was viewed as an additional cost of business, with no offsetting financial return other than accident avoidance, construction orders from many railroads followed the basic guideline of "the cheaper the better."

Consequently, numerous railroads built four-wheel bobbers. The Baltimore & Ohio had 1,200 of them by 1910; significant fleets (hundreds of cars) were also built and operated by the Western Maryland; Delaware & Hudson; Pennsylvania; Reading;

Pennsyvania's N6B cabins were among the largest single series of wood cabooses. They were rebuilt from older ND cars, and given distinctive curved-roof, angled-side cupolas. Number 981329, assigned to the Eastern Division, is at Little Creek, Va., in 1953; more than 900 were still running at the time.
H. Reid

and other railroads. Thousands were in service by the start of the 1900s.

Although four-wheel cabooses were more popular on Eastern lines, many railroads west of the Mississippi also operated them, including the Chicago, Burlington & Quincy; Rock Island; Milwaukee Road; and others. Four-wheel cars were also popular on narrow gauge and short lines, where trains were generally short and light and operated at slow speeds.

These short cabooses—with bodies typically 16 to 18 feet long and a coupled length of 21 or 22 feet—were light in weight. This could be a benefit, as added tare weight was just dead weight along for the ride. However, the light weight, when combined with the wide, stiff wheelbase of the four-wheel design, meant their riding characteristics were not ideal. As speeds increased, they tended to rock in harmonic vibration to the regular sequence of the

Chicago South Shore & South Bend had this former Pennsy wood caboose in the 1930s.
M.D. McCarter; Don Heimburger collection

New York Central no. 17404 is an ex-Big Four (Cleveland, Cincinnati, Chicago & St. Louis) caboose, one of about 350 (nos. 17350-17691) of this style. It's shorter than an NYC standard caboose (32 feet) with a tall cupola.
M.D. McCarter; Don Heimburger collection

New York Central's "standard" 19000-series cabooses are easy to spot, as their short cupolas give them a distinctive profile. Several were re-sheathed with plywood, including no. 19008, shown above in the late 1960s. It still rides on trucks with T-section cast sideframes and leaf springs. *Bob's Photo; Don Heimburger collection*

This former Michigan Central caboose shows the taller cupola used on some New York Central cars operating on the railroad's western lines. Series 17716-17839 were originally built at West Detroit from 1882 to 1914 and were rebuilt from 1925-1929. They're three feet shorter than NYC's standard design, and have four side windows. Number 17739 is at Ann Arbor, Mich., in April 1959. *Jim Hediger*

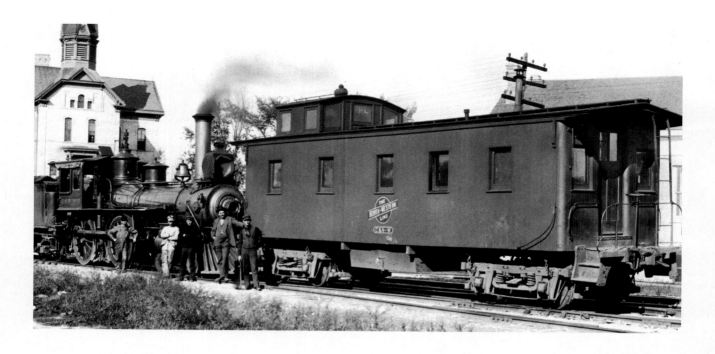

Top: As built, Chicago & North Western's common wood cabooses had five windows per side, two on each end, and three windows on the front of the cupola. Several windows would be boarded up as the cars were rebuilt over the years. This photo dates to the early 1900s. *TRAINS magazine collection*

Above: Chicago & North Western wood cabooses await their next assignments on the ready track at Proviso Yard in Chicago in 1943. Number 12010 has been rebuilt with three windows on this side, with a sliding screen over the center one. *Jack Delano, Library of Congress*

passing rail joints, giving them their nickname "bobber."

With one axle set near each car end and the journal boxes mounted in frames bolted directly to the wooden floor, they provided little vibration or shock cushioning (other than simple coil springs on some models). At more than 10 or 15 mph, four-wheelers did little but shake, rattle, and roll.

Increasing train speeds eventually sealed railroads' transition to two-truck cabooses. It was more than a comfort issue: At higher speeds their lack of suspension, light weight, and wide wheelbase made them prone to derailments and crew injuries; even minor mishaps could result in four-wheel cabooses overturning.

Railroad operating unions began pushing for legislation to ban four-wheel cabooses as a safety issue. In the 1910s, several states enacted laws requiring cabooses to be at least 24 feet in length and that they ride on two four-wheel trucks. Among the first states to act were Indiana, Minnesota, New York, North Dakota, Ohio, Washington, and Wisconsin. It was the laws in Ohio (which passed the law in 1913 with compliance required by 1919) and New York (1913) that ended most four-wheel caboose construction, as so many major railroads operated in those states.

Although most bobbers were removed from mainline service by the 1910s, there were so many of them in service that they lasted for many years on some railroads in

Chicago & North Western 10684 has been rebuilt with blanked end cupola windows, a common trait from the late 1940s onward. It retained its original five windows on this side (the other side has three). It's at Weber Yard in Evanston, Ill., in June 1958. *Henry E. Bender Jr. collection*

Chicago, Burlington & Quincy had a significant fleet of wood way-cars of similar design that lasted until the Burlington Northern merger. Number 14124 is a class NE-1 car built in the 1890s. It has a 28-foot body with three side windows. It's at Greybull, Wyo., in August 1953. *Henry E. Bender Jr. collection*

switching and local services (and in mainline service in some states where their use hadn't been banned). Many were eventually rebuilt into two-truck cars. Among the last four-wheel cabooses constructed were a half-dozen Lehigh & New England cars built by AC&F in 1914 (which remained in local service into the 1950s) and Pacific Electric,

which built eight bobbers in 1921 (these also ran through the 1950s).

Probably the best known four-wheel cars were Pennsylvania's large fleet of class NC and ND cars, most of which were eventually rebuilt with steel underframes and stretched bodies as N6A and N6B cars starting in 1914 (more on those in a bit). As the photo on

page 34 shows, however, some ND cabooses remained in service into the 1940s and even later in local service.

Conventional cabooses

At speeds over 25 mph, the use of two trucks, each equipped with two axles and spring suspension, was slowly accepted as necessary to give the conductor's car adequate control for a tolerable ride. Such was necessary for the conductor to write wheel reports, or review his orders or the employee timetable. Longer body length (25 to 30 feet), also allowed more room for bunks—becoming necessary as runs increased in length and crews found themselves staying nights away from their

A Burlington Northern transfer run rolls past 21st Street in Chicago in early 1971. Caboose 13945 was built by Chicago, Burlington & Quincy's Aurora (Ill.) shops in 1912. The nearly 60-year old car is part of class NE-7. It's trailing BN SW1000 435 and a former CB&Q GP7.
Russ Porter; Don Heimburger collection

home bases—and ample equipment storage.

All-wood construction remained common into the 1900s, but steel underframes came into wide use by 1914. Many older cabooses were eventually rebuilt with steel underframes or center sills.

Construction styles continued to vary widely among railroads and builders, with little of the standardization that would eventually occur with steel caboose designs after World War II. Whether built by railroads' own shops or an outside builder, cabooses generally followed each railroad's own design (albeit with updates and detail variations).

Railroad designs

Let's look at several of the most common and best-known wood caboose designs of major railroads.

Possibly the largest single class of wood cabooses was Pennsylvania's N6, with more than 1,200 built from 1914 to 1923. Most were rebuilt from four-wheel cabooses that—although not old—were largely obsolete because of safety concerns and new state laws restricting their use. Their rebuilding coincided with the building of new all-steel class N5 cabooses, mainly for PRR's eastern lines (more on those in Chapter 3), with the wood N6 cars intended for western lines.

The rebuilds kept their wood bodies, but atop steel frames. The body was lengthened by adding to one end (causing the cupola to be slightly off center) with a distinctive curved-roof cupola, which had a steeper curve than the caboose roof itself. The series had two subclasses: N6A cars had cupolas with vertical sides; N6B cars had angled sides. The N6B was far more common, and many N6A cars were eventually rebuilt with angled side walls. These cars had long lives: More than 800 were still in service in the late 1950s, and some survived into the Penn Central merger of 1968.

The other major Northeastern carrier,

Left: Chicago, Burlington & Quincy no. X14644 is a class NE-4 car, built around 1900. It's 30 feet long with four side windows, and has the single side cupola window common to Burlington cabooses. The railroad's wood waycars rode on passenger-style beam trucks.
Henry E. Bender Jr.; Don Heimburger collection

41

Santa Fe's early wood cabooses lacked end platforms, instead having side doors with steps and ladders of grab irons. Most were out of service by the 1930s, but some lasted in local service another two decades. Number 1038, built by the railroad in the 1910s, is at Brownwood, Texas, in February 1952. *Bob's Photo*

The 1300-1449 class of cabooses, built by American Car & Foundry in 1923, were the last wood cabooses bought by Santa Fe, but they introduced the basic design that would continue through the end of the caboose era. They had four windows on one side and three on the other. Number 1426 has just been repainted and reconditioned in 1952. *TRAINS magazine collection*

New York Central, settled on a standard design in the early 1900s after acquiring and operating several caboose designs of predecessor and subsidiary lines. From 1912 to 1924, the railroad rebuilt many older cabooses and built new ones in the same style. These distinctive cars measured 35 feet long across the end sills and were characterized by their wood sheathing, three side windows, visible ends of the I-section cross bearers, visible truss rods (left in place even on cars with steel underframes), and squatty, short cupolas that were offset toward one end.

The bulk of these cabooses were 19000-series cars built for NYC proper from

Southern Pacific no. 550, shown in its builder's photo, is a class CA caboose built in 1907. These cabooses had four side windows, a slanted-side, offset cupola with two windows on each wall, wood underframes (originally without truss rods), and rode on archbar trucks with leaf springs. *Trains magazine collection*

Number 181 is from class C-30-1, the most-common type of Espee caboose. It has a steel frame and the roof-width, vertical-side cupola used on many of these cars. *M.D. McCarter; Don Heimburger collection*

The CA-1 class was Union Pacific's most-common wood caboose. It has three side windows and an angled-side, offset cupola. The ends of the side bearers and bolsters are visible under the side, as is the KC (combined) brake reservoir and cylinder between the trucks. Number 2601 is in fresh yellow paint at Ault, Colo., in November 1947. *Henry E. Bender Jr. collection*

Illinois Central no. 9339 is from the railroad's largest group of wood cars, 225 28-foot cabooses (nos. 9151-9375) built in 1923. They had traditional-style sliding windows and widely off-set cupolas. Some, like this one, had side doors. The IC's later steel cars would follow a similar design. *Don Heimburger collection*

Rock Island's standard wood caboose, built from 1905-1921 (nos. 17900-18807), had four or five side windows, running boards around the cupola, and a horizontal fascia board along the top of each side. Most, as 18096 (here in 1938), were eventually rebuilt and reconditioned and many served into the 1960s. *TRAINS magazine collection*

Rock Island's signature cabooses of the late steam to early diesel period were 180 single-sheathed 35-foot cars rebuilt from old boxcars from 1938-1944. Number 17667 has been restricted to yard service by this 1970s view. *Don Heimburger collection*

Western Pacific 612 was rebuilt from an old single-sheathed boxcar in 1937; it's shown in September 1937. Note the archbar trucks even at this late date. The WP rebuilt 38 cabooses (nos. 605-644) this way from 1937 to 1942; the railroad built several bay window cars in the same manner (see Chapter 5). *W.C. Whittaker*

Soo Line's 34-foot wood cars served the railroad from 1906 into the 1970s, albeit with rebuilding. The cars retained archbar trucks until retirement. They had cupolas with two or one (car at right) side windows. Number 229 is freshly repainted in this April 1964 scene at North Fond du Lac, Wis. *Russ Porter; Don Heimburger collection*

The Duluth, South Shore & Atlantic had a fleet of wood cabooses that went to Soo Line following their 1961 merger. Number 595 is on the rear of a train at Ewin, Mich., in September 1963. *Ray Buhrmaster; Don Heimburger collection*

Early Wabash wood cabooses in the 2000 series, built around 1900, had unique arched cupola roofs, wide fascia/letter boards along the tops of the sides, and archbar trucks. Number 2229, shown in 1982, has been restored by the National Museum of Transportation in St. Louis. *Don Heimburger*

The Wabash's newer 2600-series cabooses—built from 1925-1929—had cupola roofs with flatter curves. They also lacked the side fascia board of the earlier cars. *D. Smith; Don Heimburger collection*

Nickel Plate's 1000-series wood cabooses, built from the 1880s through 1924, had tall centered cupolas with single side windows and side-mounted signal indicators. They had long service lives, with many eventually wearing NKP's flashy "high speed service" scheme. Number 1103 is at Charleston, Ill., in September 1965, a year after the Norfolk & Western merger. *Clayton Tanner; Don Heimburger collection*

A former Nickel Plate wood caboose has been freshly painted in Norfolk & Western colors after the 1964 merger. Number 559023 leads a transfer run (with a switcher still in NKP lettering) across the diamonds at Pullman Junction (Chicago) in April 1965. The ex-NKP cabooses became class C-11 on the N&W. *Chuck Zeiler; Don Heimburger collection*

Northern Pacific 1741 is one of 90 cabooses built by Pacific Car & Foundry in 1921 (1700-1789). It has a 24-foot body (30 feet over end sills) and a tall end cupola with single side window. It's still in service at Cloquet, Minn., in the late 1960s. The basic design was used for other series of NP cabooses as well.
D. Smith; Don Heimburger collection

Spokane, Portland & Seattle nos. 850-855 were among the last wood-body cabooses built. They were turned out by parent Great Northern at its St. Cloud, Minn., shops in 1946. They were 36 feet long over end sills and stood 14'-6¾" to the cupola roof. Number 854 awaits its next assignment in February 1962.
Merk Hobson

1902-1923. Cars in the 17000s and 18000s are often shorter, or of varying designs from subsidiary lines, and may have differing window patterns. Taller cupolas were used on some cabooses designed for use on NYC's western lines. Most served through the 1950s, but their retirements increased as the NYC began acquiring large numbers of new steel bay window cabooses into the 1960s. About 190 NYC wood cars survived into the

Penn Central merger in 1968.

The Chicago & North Western had several hundred wood cars built to a common design, with vertical sheathing, peaked roofs, and five windows per side. The cupolas were offset, with straight sides, curved roofs, and two windows on each side and end. They rode on passenger-style (beam) trucks. Cars built from the 1890s until 1913 were all wood (with visible truss

Great Northern operated several small wood cabooses (24-foot bodies; 33 feet over end sills) built in the 1910s. Number X617 is in yard service at Vancouver, B.C., in 1957.
Bob's Photo; Don Heimburger collection

During World War II, Great Northern built 50 plywood-sheathed cabooses at its St. Cloud, Minn., shops. They had 30-foot bodies and followed the same design as the railroad's contemporary steel cars. Here no. X244 poses for a publicity photo with a string of new plywood-sheathed boxcars in 1944. *Great Northern*

Duluth, Missabe & Iron Range C-12 was built as a four-wheel caboose in 1894 by Duluth Manufacturing Co. for Duluth, Missabe & Northern. It has a 24-foot body, channel side sills with angled ends, fascia board, and end cupola with slightly slanted sides. It was rebuilt with two trucks in 1910, and it's shown here at Proctor, Minn., in 1950. *Henry J. McCord*

Norfolk & Western's most-common wood car was the CF class, 381 cars (518000-518380) built from 1914 to 1924. Their vertical sheathing continued from the cupola sides downward through the car side without a break. Number 518007 is at Norfolk, Va., in March 1968. *Dennis Schmidt collection*

rods); steel underframes were used on cars built from 1913 to 1928.

Older cars were rebuilt and reconditioned from 1919 through 1937, with steel center and end sills added to truss-rod cars. The most visible modifications were to windows: cars wound up with four or five on one side and three on the other, and cupola end windows were often planked over.

The original cars were numbered in the 1500s-2200s and 4800s-4900s; rebuilt cars received numbers in the 11400s to 12400s. Many survived through the 1950s (some were converted to bay window cars), but as new steel bay window cars arrived in the 1950s-1960s, they were retired.

The Chicago, Burlington & Quincy was another Western railroad with a large group

At first glance, this Central of Georgia car resembles the N&W CF class, with car sides that continue to the cupola sides. The CofG car has tall-mounted side windows, cast platform steps, and a 28-foot body. It's one of 80 similar cars built by the railroad from 1922-1937 (originally 31501-31580; surviving cars were renumbered X1-X74 in 1942). It's at Sylacauga, Ala., in April 1952. *Henry E. Bender Jr. collection*

The Southern Railway had a significant fleet of wood cabooses built in the early 1900s. Number X2286 is one of 400 cars built from 1914 to 1917 (nos. X2026-X2425), many of which were later rebuilt and ran through the 1950s. They have peaked car and cupola roofs and metal-angle cupola braces that extend to the car side. *M.D. McCarter; Don Heimburger collection*

Gulf, Mobile & Ohio no. 2868, built in 1914, is one of many similar cars built into the 1920s for predecessor Mobile & Ohio; 57 of these cars survived the GM&O merger in 1940 (nos. 2847-2893). The center-cupola, peaked-roof car is at Artesia, Miss., in January 1972.
Martin O'Toole

Atlantic Coast Line's most-numerous wood cabooses were the more than 450 cars of class M-3, which were built new or rebuilt from older cars from 1922 to 1927. The 30-foot-body cars originally had vertical tongue-and-groove siding, but many were later re-sheathed with plywood. Number 0323, built in June 1925, poses after receiving Weldwood Duraply sheathing in June 1962.
U.S. Plywood Corp.

of similar-design wood cars that lasted a long time in service. The railroad built nearly 900 cars in classes NE-1 to NE-9 from the late 1880s through 1925 at several of its shops (mainly Aurora for later cars). Some early cars were 28 feet long, but most were 30-footers with four side windows and offset cupolas with single windows on the sides and two on the front and back. They rode on passenger-style trucks.

The Q kept its wood cabooses maintained very well, and most enjoyed long service lives—34 class NE-4 cars, built before 1902, lasted into the 1970s under Burlington Northern. Even through the 1960s, they could often be seen in high-speed mainline service—the passenger trucks provided a smooth ride.

Early Santa Fe wood cabooses lacked end platforms. They had end cupolas and side doors with steps that were located just toward the center from the cupola. The first two main groups were built by AC&F. The

1906-built cars (nos. 540-618) had grab-iron ladders on each end and on one end of each side. The next series, 619-772, had the side grab-iron ladders next to the door. The railroad then built a series of similar cars starting in 1911 (806-1060).

In 1922, American Car & Foundry delivered 150 cars (nos. 1122-1171) to the basic end-cupola style that the railroad would be known for. These were followed by perhaps the AT&SF's best-known class of wood cabooses, the 1300-1449 class, 150 cars built by American Car & Foundry in 1923. They introduced the basic body style that would be used on the later steel cars—which is fitting, as the first orders of those were also from AC&F. The cars were 28 feet long and delivered with three windows on one side and two on the other, with two windows on each side of the cupola (all of which could be opened). The cupola was near the end of the car, and had vertical side walls. The bodies and cupolas had radial roofs (sheathed in

Seaboard Air Line operated several cabooses of this 36-foot, offset-cupola design built by Magor and American Car & Foundry through the 1920s. Number 5407, built in 1925, is looking good at Fort Lauderdale, Fla., in February 1966. *Dennis Schmidt collection*

smooth tin). They rode on archbar trucks. Many lasted in service into the 1950s and even the 1960s, but were retired as newer steel cars arrived.

Southern Pacific's CA cabooses, built just after the turn of the century (and before 1910), were designed under Harriman control and thus share a common appearance with Union Pacific's CA class. They have four windows per side and sloped-side, off-center cupolas. They were built with wood underframes with no truss rods and ride on archbar trucks. Most had truss rods added by the early 1920s.

In 1914 the SP began building cabooses with riveted steel underframes. The resulting class C-30-1 cars, built through 1928, became the largest group of cabooses on the railroad (more than 600 built). Early cars had slanted-side cupolas; later cars (and many rebuilt earlier cars) received full-width straight-sided cupolas. Later variations included the C-30-2 and C-30-3 in 1929-1930. The C30-3 can be spotted by its visible side sill, with the bottoms of the side trusses visible below the wood side sheathing.

Union Pacific's standard caboose of the early 1900s was the CA, which—as a Harriman railroad—matched SP's design. The UP bought 350 of them from 1907 to 1913 (including those on UP subsidiary railroads). The UP's "modern" wood car was the CA-1, acquired from 1913-1924 by various builders, and following SP's C30-1 design. It was the railroad's largest class of wood cabooses (380 including subsidiaries), and had a steel underframe, slanted-side cupola, and three windows per side. They were the final wood cabooses bought by UP. Most were retired by the mid-1960s.

The Illinois Central started building offset-cupola wood cars with 28-foot bodies in 1915. Its Centralia shops turned out 450 similar cars (9001-9450) in six series through 1929, plus another 100 non-cupola cars in 1936. Many ran into the 1960s; the railroad's

Several former Baltimore & Ohio class I-1 cabooses were eventually assigned to Baltimore & Ohio Chicago Terminal and renumbered. Class I-1A C1896 has received Andrews caboose trucks, replacing the original archbars. Crewmen are ready to couple it to a train at Barr Yard in Blue Island, Ill., in the late 1940s.
Trains magazine collection

Baltimore & Ohio built 401 cars to this basic design as class I-5 starting in 1924. Number C2087 reflects an as-built car with archbar trucks, horizontal brake wheels on the end platforms, and short (15-foot) truck spacing. An upgraded I-5D car can be seen on page 29. *Baltimore & Ohio*

Most of the lettering has peeled off of Chesapeake & Ohio caboose 90903, which was built in 1929 and shown here around 1940. It has a straight-side cupola that's slightly off center and two side windows with brackets holding sliding screens. *M.D. McCarter; Don Heimburger collection*

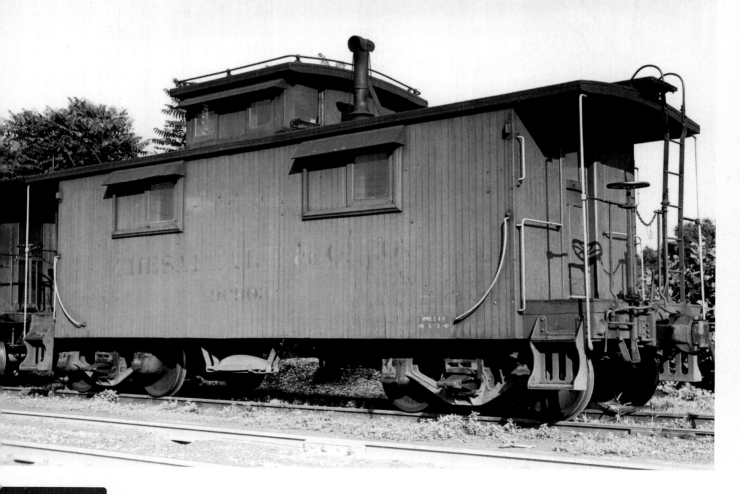

This C&O 90800-series caboose has been reconditioned, with the original window screen brackets removed. It's at Bay City, Mich., in January 1968. *Dennis Schmidt; Don Heimburger collection*

Boston & Maine no. C90 is one of five wood-body, steel-underframe cabooses built by Magor in 1931 for Lehigh & New England (L&NE nos. 574-578). It follows the basic design of earlier USRA cabooses (see page 107). The B&M acquired it after L&NE ceased operations in 1961; it sports a fresh McGinnis paint scheme and new window screens in October 1962. *Frank DiFalco*

later steel cars followed a similar design starting in 1940.

Single-sheathed cabooses (sometimes called "outside braced") were common on the Rock Island and Western Pacific, both of which built them from older single-sheathed boxcars. They were distinctive with their visible outside truss-style framing and horizontal plank sheathing inside the framing. The Rock built 200 cabooses in its Chicago shops from 1938-1944. Most were

standard cupola cabooses (nos. 17625-17699, 17725-17764, 17785-17849), but 20 (17765-17784) were longer, with center baggage doors, for branch line service. The standard cabooses were 35'-1" over end sills and 15'-3" tall to the cupola roof.

The Western Pacific built several cabooses starting with old single-sheathed Pullman-Standard boxcars from 1937 to 1942, numbering them 605-644 (omitting no. 629; there were two 619s, the second replacing

The Grand Trunk Western was a Canadian National subsidiary, and its paint scheme, numbering, and many construction details follow that of its parent railroad. Caboose no. 77049 is a wood-body, end-cupola car that still rides on archbar trucks in this August 1959 photo at South Bend, Ind.
Dennis Schmidt; Don Heimburger collection

The Central Vermont was another Canadian National subsidiary. Number 4001, built in 1914, has been refurbished, upgraded with leaf-spring caboose trucks, and is in good shape at New London, Conn., in February 1973.
Dennis Schmidt collection

Canadian Pacific's standard wood cabooses featured distinctive tall, end-mounted cupolas. The 35-foot-long cars were 15'-2" tall to the top of the cupola roof. Number 438527 is at Sault St. Marie, Ontario, in July 1965. *Dennis Schmidt collection*

Canadian National's standard wood cabooses stood 14'-5" tall, with 30-foot bodies (35 feet long overall) and end cupolas with a lower profile than Canadian Pacific cabooses. Number 78317 was built in the 1920s and has just been refurbished in this company photo from 1942. *Canadian National*

Denver & Rio Grande Western operated several styles of narrow gauge cabooses. Long-frame (26-foot) end-cupola caboose 04343 was rebuilt from an older boxcar in 1914. It trails a steam locomotive in August 1965. *Chris Burritt; Don Heimburger collection*

a wrecked car). Starting in 1942 the WP switched to bay window cars for its rebuilds.

The Soo Line relied on wood cars later than most other railroads, rebuilding and reconditioning them until wide-cupola steel International cars arrived in the 1960s. The most common design were 133 34-foot cars built by American Car & Foundry and the railroad itself from 1906 to 1913. They eventually received steel underframes (but retained truss rods). They had three windows on one side and one on the other; cupola sides had one or two windows. Soo cabooses were numbered in the 100s and 200s; 20 cabooses assigned to its Wisconsin Central subsidiary had five-digit numbers starting with "99."

In the Northeast and New England, cabooses often have shorter bodies (24 to 28 feet) and frames and shorter, centered cupolas.

Baltimore & Ohio relied heavily on four-wheel cabooses into the 1900s. Although the railroad had several earlier eight-wheel cars built starting in 1886, the I-1 (built from 1913-1918, 303 cars, nos. C5-C399 and C1615-C1624, not all numbers used) and I-1A cars (built 1922-1923, C400-C499) were the first system standard cars. The 24-foot-body cars had four (four-pane) windows per side, with peaked roofs and peaked-roof cupolas with vertical side walls. They originally had archbar trucks.

In 1924, the B&O began building its successor, the I-5, turning out 401 cars (nos. C1900-C2299; there was one wreck replacement). This distinctive car had four single-pane windows and a centered cupola with angled side walls and peaked roof, steel underframe, steel ends, wood-sheathed sides, and archbar trucks. A key modification was the wheelbase: The initial 15-foot wheelbase proved dangerously unstable when being pushed, so many cars were modified by stretching the wheelbase to 19 feet, which required narrowing the end platforms

(additional weight was also added). These became I-5c or I-5D cars, which can be spotted by their narrowed platforms and the bolsters that were pushed out farther toward the ends (see page 29 in Chapter 1). Other modifications over the years included cast trucks, vertically mounted brake wheels, and side-mounted oil filler pipes and toilet vents. Some were eventually re-sheathed with plywood. Some lasted in service until the 1980s.

The Chesapeake & Ohio acquired several series of wood cabooses starting in the 1910s that all had a similar family appearance. Cabooses in the 90401, 90600, 90700, 90800, and 90900 series had 25-foot wood bodies, slightly offset cupolas, and two windows per side (each of which had a rectangular bracket to hold a sliding screen).

Other railroads running similar wood cabooses included Boston & Maine; Delaware & Hudson; Pittsburg & Shawmut; and others.

Canada

Canadian Pacific's classic wood caboose design goes back to about 1905. They were distinctive, with tall cupolas located toward the end. Many series were built until 1945 with the same basic dimensions: 35-foot cars that stood 15'-2" to the top of the cupola roof. Beginning in 1912 steel center sills were used. Many were rebuilt in the 1960s and '70s with plywood sides. On the side were three windows and the cupola had eight windows. As they were rebuilt beginning in the mid 1920s, one side window in the cupola was boarded over, the third side window was removed, and the center window in the cupola end was sheeted over. The steps were changed to a longer design and the end railings increased in height. Some of these cars survived through the 1970s and into the 1980s.

Canadian National had hundreds of end-cupola wood cabooses built to a standard design from the 1920s into the 1940s. Many

Four-wheel cabooses were popular with narrow-gauge railroads. Colorado & Southern 1009 is a three-foot-gauge car built as Denver, Leadville & Gunnison 1516 in the late 1800s. It then became C&S 312, then in 1911 was renumbered 1009. It has a single side window and an end cupola with two windows on each side. *Don Heimburger collection*

were rebuilt from older boxcars; others were built new. These cars had 30-foot bodies (35-foot overall length) and stood 14'-5" tall to the top of the cupola, giving them a different appearance compared to CP's cars.

Narrow gauge

Most narrow gauge cabooses through the start of the 1900s featured all-wood construction, including framing and underframes. The construction techniques were similar to standard gauge cars, but on a smaller scale: cars were typically about 6'-6" wide, compared to 9 to 10 feet for standard gauge. Four-wheel cars were common through the 1880s, but as with standard gauge lines, they moved to two-truck (eight-wheel) cars by the 1890s and early 1900s.

Cabooses followed many designs, even on individual railroads. Cars were turned out in small lots, and many times were rebuilt from older cabooses or freight cars. Many cars built in the late 1800s lasted through the demise of narrow gauge railroads.

Transition to steel

The Pennsylvania Railroad started the move to all-steel cabooses in 1914. Although plenty of wood-body cabooses were still built in the following years, by the 1920s most construction turned to steel. Notable exceptions were several wood cars built during World War II because of restrictions on steel use—these often followed existing steel-car designs.

Even for wood cars with steel framing and underframes, wood sheathing was subject to deterioration from exposure to weather. Rain (which all too easily penetrated bodies at joints such as window frames) and sun alike led to peeling paint and rotting wood. Sheathing required frequent painting, repair, and replacement. Plywood proved to be even less resistant to weather damage than conventional tongue-and-groove boards.

Wood cars began to be retired in large numbers as caboose fleets shrunk through the 1950s and new steel cars arrived. However, as the photos in this chapter show, many wood cars served into the 1960s and some survived into the 1980s thanks to rebuilding and reconditioning programs.

A single-sheathed wood cupola caboose carries the markers for a short steam-powered National of Mexico narrow gauge train at Puebla (southeast of Mexico City) in November 1966.
Henry E. Bender Jr.;
Don Heimburger collection

Chapter 3

Steel

Brand-new Great Northern steel caboose no. X52 trails a freight train through Fargo, N.D., in August 1962. The caboose is one of 15 (nos. X51-65) in the series built at the railroad's St. Cloud (Minn.) shops earlier in the year. The welded 31-foot car was among the last road cabooses built by the GN; it would turn to International Car Co. for future orders. *Russ Porter; Don Heimburger collection*

cabooses

SAFETY AND DURABILITY MADE STEEL CONSTRUCTION THE STANDARD BY THE 1920s

Although Henry Bessemer patented his steel-making process in 1856, it wasn't until after the Civil War that steel began to significantly replace iron and masonry in general or railroad construction. The rails themselves were the first major railroad use for steel beginning in the 1870s. As steel-framed buildings and bridges multiplied across America, it was only a matter of time before railcars followed suit.

The crew of Pennsy N5B 477783 in April 1954 pushes their cabin to get it rolling downgrade at Altoona (Pa.) Yard. They will then ride it to a stop. Note the large vertical collision posts on the end. *Wayne Leeman*

Pennsylvania's N5c cabooses are spotted by the porthole windows and streamlined cupolas. Number 477947 is at Saginaw, Mich., in 1968. *Dennis Schmidt; Don Heimburger collection*

Pennsy's last new cabin cars were the 200 cars of class N8. They returned to rectangular windows, and were longer than earlier cars (note the wide platforms). The long rail on the roof is the antenna for PRR's train-phone system; the two circular fixtures on the roof at right are receiving coils for the system. *Pennsylvania Railroad*

The first all-steel passenger car was constructed in the 1890s, followed by the first all-steel Pullman, the *Jamestown*, in 1908. Freight cars of various kinds followed, first with hopper and tank cars, and eventually flatcars and boxcars by the early 1900s. Even by the late 1910s, although steel center sills and underframes were coming into wide use, carbodies typically remained wood (or wood sheathing over a steel frame). When the United States Railroad Administration (USRA) issued several standard designs for freight cars during World War I, its caboose design was a wood body atop a steel frame. However, the Pennsylvania Railroad had already begun an extensive program of building all-steel cabooses (in 1914), and other railroads would follow suit after the war.

By the 1920s, most new cabooses featured all-steel construction. The cost of steel cars had become competitive as builders and railroad shops began building cars on a larger scale, with fabricated components and mass-production techniques, and steel became the preferred choice because it was far more durable and long lasting.

Steel bodies were typically riveted

Many former PRR cabooses made it into the Conrail era. Here N5c 23066 is in fresh Conrail blue paint (with black roof) in September 1976 at Abrams Yard in Norristown, Pa. *J. David Ingles*

through the 1940s, with sides and ends comprising steel sheets riveted together over a steel frame. Roofs could be radial (rounded) or peaked, and were often wood bases or other cross bracing covered in sheets of flat steel sheathing, riveted together. By the 1940s, panel roofs (as used on boxcars) became more common. These were sectional with raised patterns (first rectangular, then diagonal, then X-pattern) for strength, and they didn't require separate bracing

This former Pennsylvania N5 caboose, built in 1927, is at Bay City, Mich., on Detroit & Mackinac in June 1976. It retains much of its original appearance, but has received new sealed windows, modified freight-car trucks, and AB brakes.
Dennis Schmidt; Don Heimburger collection

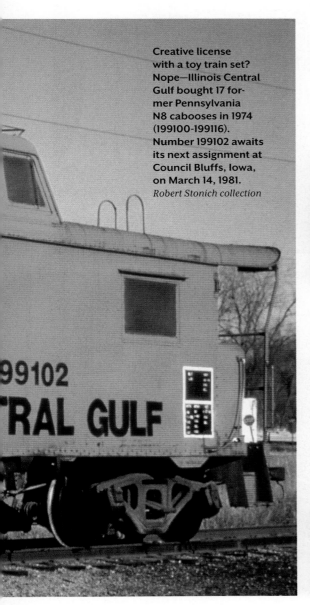

or support. These panels had raised caps between them that secured them and made them weathertight.

Cupolas, as with wood cars, could be centered or offset to various extremes. Cupola side and end walls could be vertical or angled inward; the sides could have one or two windows. As with the body roof, the cupola roof could be rounded or peaked. Cupola placement, size (height and length), and style remain key identifying features.

Window design was upgraded, with metal frames and sashes and improved seals. Gone were the multi-pane wood-framed windows with muntins. As with wood cars, window size, style, and placement are key spotting features.

Interiors of early steel cabooses didn't change much. Initially, most steel caboose interiors were finished in tongue-and-groove cut softwood (pine or spruce), just as with wood cars. Generally, you couldn't tell a 1920s or '30s steel caboose from its wooden predecessor by viewing the interior, as they were virtually identical. Coal still fueled the pot-bellied stove (which was flat-topped

Top: Santa Fe no. 2171R, built in 1943, has a radial roof. The "R" is for radio, with a frame-mounted generator and antenna on a flat plate on the cupola roof. It's at Belen, N.M., in July 1967. *Henry E. Bender Jr. collection*

Above: From the 1920s to the 1950s, Santa Fe used "wig wags" or "highballers" on many cabooses to signal the head end. You're looking at the rear of the near wig wag. *Robert O. Hale; M.D. McCarter collection*

Number 999244, here in 1984, was built in 1947 and rebuilt in 1967 as part of Santa Fe's first group of rebuilt cabooses, class CE-1. Several body windows have been plated over, with one new sealed window. There's also a toilet vent (on the side to the left of the cupola), water filler on the end, wipers on the cupola end windows, a built-in marker light, and exterior lights at all four corners. *Don Heimburger collection*

The yellow-painted cupola indicates that Santa Fe 999624 is in local or assigned service. The CE-3 cars received limited rebuilding; several windows were plated over, but the remaining windows are original. The peaked-roof car has a panel roof; it was built in 1949, rebuilt in 1968, and is shown here in April 1978. *Don Heimburger collection*

for cooking), illumination was provided by kerosene lamps, a wood conductor's desk and chair was in one corner, toilets were non-existant or rudimentary, and there were multiple bunks, including a couple of fold-down ones, for crews to catch sleep when away from their home yards.

Modernization

By the 1950s, as with other freight cars, welded construction became more common. Steel running boards replaced wood in the 1940s. Early cast solid-bearing trucks (Andrews and others) gave way to more modern designs, with roller-bearing leaf-spring trucks becoming common by the 1960s.

Radio communication first appeared in the 1940s and became common by the 1950s (see page 97). With radio came a need for electricity, provided by axle-driven generators that charged onboard batteries. With electricity came the move to electric marker lamps and interior electric lighting. Oil-fired stoves and heaters replaced coal versions. Wood interiors gave way to steel

Santa Fe rebuilt three peaked-roof (1949-built) cabooses in 1969 without cupolas for ore-train service based at Hurley, N.M.; eliminating the cupola allowed cars to fit through a rotary dumper. Classified CE-4, no. 999637 trails a string of empty ore cars near Hurley in September 1979. *Don Heimburger collection*

Union Pacific CA-3 caboose no. 3721 sports a full-side slogan during a safety campaign in August 1953. The car is from the first group of UP steel cupola cabooses, riveted cars built by Mt. Vernon in 1942. It's had its original wood-beam trucks replaced with outside-hanger trucks. *Union Pacific*

Members of the rear-end crew are on the platform as their eastbound Union Pacific intermodal train heads into the siding at Stockton, Calif., clearing the main for a westbound. It's November 1982, twilight for caboose operations on the UP—and railroads across the country. *Steve Schmollinger*

or composite material (Met-L-Wood, a sandwich of plywood encased in thin sheets of metal, was common), and safety features became more important, with additional interior grab irons and guardrails, desks and other fixtures with rounded corners and edges, and recessed steps.

Toilets became mandatory per union agreements by the late 1950s (look for external roof- or side-mounted vents). A rise in vandalism meant a reduction in windows,

with sealed safety-glass windows becoming more common by the 1960s (and required on all new/rebuilt cabooses as of 1980 and on all cars in 1984), with many window openings simply plated over.

By the 1960s, the efficiency of pool arrangements, elimination of many conductor-assigned cars, and other factors had reduced the number of cabooses needed. There were about 25,000 cabooses on U.S. railroads in 1950; in 1960, this was down to

International Car Co. built Union Pacific's 100 class CA-9 cars in 1967. They share the same basic appearance of UP's earlier cars, but have welded bodies and a slightly longer wheelbase. The large "P" indicates the car is equipped for pool service. *Don Heimburger collection*

Illinois Central operated more than 300 steel side-door cabooses in mainline service. Number 9724 is from the original series of 100 cars built by IC's Centralia shops in 1940, using frames of old gondolas. It's at Chicago in July 1962. *Russ Porter, Don Heimburger collection*

As with IC, Illinois Central Gulf stenciled cabooses' assigned territories on the sides, in this case "Chicago-New Orleans." Number 199948 was built at Centralia in 1950 and is shown here in the early 1980s. *Trains magazine collection*

The New Haven decked out one of its signature NE-5 steel cabooses with a signboard to publicize its Trailiner piggyback service in 1954. The rounded roof edges and vertical weld seams make the cars easy to identify. The conductor gives a staged highball signal from the back platform as the train prepares for departure in New York City. *New Haven*

Boston & Maine had Pullman-Standard build 20 cabooses to the same design as the New Haven NE-5s. Number C10 has had screens added over the side and cupola windows in this late 1970s view. The weathering shows the vertical stiffeners. *M.D. McCarter collection*

The Chicago Great Western bought 25 NE-5 design cabooses from Pullman-Standard in 1945-1946. You can see the outline of the old logo that's been painted over behind the "CGW" lettering in this early 1970s view following the merger with Chicago & North Western. *M.D. McCarter; Don Heimburger collection*

18,337 (plus another 2,500 or so in Canada). This meant most older wood cabooses were retired; early steel cabooses were sometimes rebuilt. That decade saw an increased number of advanced caboose designs placed in service, as railroads moved away from standard-cupola cars toward bay window or wide-cupola designs (see Chapter 5).

As with wood cabooses, most early steel designs were unique to individual railroads. A notable exception was the so-called "Northeastern" caboose, designed by the Reading and copied by several other railroads. Those are covered in depth in Chapter 4. We'll start with a look at several railroads' distinctive designs, then look at

some common later designs developed starting in the 1950s, as caboose technology improved and International Car Co. began dominating the caboose market.

Railroad designs

The Pennsylvania Railroad, in keeping with its self-proclaimed status as "The Standard Railroad of the World," was the first to begin building a fleet of new steel cabin cars (its name for cabooses) in 1914. The class N5 cars (see page 199) would indeed become a standard, with more than 600 built (nos. 477000-477619) through 1941. They were readily identifiable by their long, centered (angled-side) cupolas, steel roof that

Number 90329 is from the last batch of standard-cupola steel cabooses bought by the Chesapeake & Ohio. It was built by American Car & Foundry in 1949 for the railroad's PM District (former Pere Marquette lines).
Chesapeake & Ohio

wrapped around the tops of the sides, and rectangular windows at the end of each side. They measured 28'-11½" over end sills. Most eventually received "collision posts"—a pair of heavy vertical beams at each end. They originally rode on archbar trucks (specifically for the PRR, 2A-F1 trucks), but most eventually received cast trucks; early versions

had K brakes, later cars had AB brakes.

These were followed by class N5B, 200 cars built with these improvements in 1941 (477620-477819). Another visual change was moving the stove from a corner to a space next to the cupola, resulting in the smoke jack moving as well.

The distinctive follow-up was the class

Chesapeake & Ohio no. 90070 was built by Magor in 1941. These had angled cupolas, two side windows, and a prominent horizontal rivet strip along the side. The railroad acquired more than 400 cabooses to the same basic design from three builders from 1937 through 1949.
H. Reid

In 1969 and 1970, Chesapeake & Ohio rebuilt more than 180 older cabooses, stripping the interiors and adding new fixtures, new windows, and roller-bearing trucks. Note the filler pipe for the new oil heater at right as well as the electric marker lamps. Number 3583 is at Greenville, Mich., in May 1974. *Dennis Schmidt; Don Heimburger collection*

The first 70 steel cabooses on the Wabash (nos. 2700-2769) were a conventional style, with riveted bodies, radial roof, and a tall cupola with straight sides and rounded roof. Number 2740 was painted red and white with blue lettering in the early 1960s. *Don Heimburger*

Wabash's streamlined-cupola cabooses had bodies similar to the previous standard cabooses, but cupolas that angled inward on all four sides. Cupola side windows slid open on external tracks. The cabooses also had panel roofs. Number 2799 wears the red and white scheme at Tilton, Ill., in April 1967, three years after the Wabash was merged into Norfolk & Western. *Don Heimburger collection*

Ann Arbor no. 2832, built in 1955, was one of 17 (nos. 2830-2846) cabooses nearly identical to the Wabash stream-lined-cupola cars. The AA cars had steel end doors (Wabash ver-sions had wood doors). Number 2832 is at Owosso, Mich., in August 1978. *Jim Hediger*

When the Wabash was merged into the Norfolk & Western in 1964, the streamlined cabooses were part of the deal. They became nos. 562770-562859 in N&W class C-18, wearing several paint schemes into the 1980s. Number 562842 is freshly painted in red at Bellevue, Ohio, in April 1979. *Ed Durnwald; James Gillum collection*

N5c car, introduced in 1942 with 200 built (nos. 477820-478019). These had pairs of round porthole windows at the end of each side (plus two on each end, as well as on the end doors), along with angled cupola ends for a more-streamlined look. They measured 30'-7" over their end sills.

The railroad's last new cabin cars were the 200 class N8 cars built in 1950-1951 (nos. 478020-478219). These were longer than earlier cars (33'-2" over end sills), and went back to rectangular side windows (which were wider than on the N5 cars).

Paint and lettering schemes varied through the years. A distinctive variation

was the yellow cupolas on some cars, which indicated they were in east-west pool service. Many of these PRR cabooses survived into the Penn Central (1968) and Conrail (1976) eras to wear green and blue (and CR maintenance gray). Second-hand Pennsy cabooses could also be found on several railroads, including Detroit & Mackinac and Illinois Central Gulf.

If the Pennsylvania's were the most-recognizable Eastern designs, certainly the most recognizable Western caboose was the end-cupola steel caboose of Santa Fe. The first 150 were built by AC&F in 1927 with another 100 in 1928 and 125 in 1929 (nos.

1500-1874) and 22 in 1931 (1979-2000). All had radial roofs; early cars had K brakes and horizontal end brake wheels, later changed to AB brakes and vertical brake wheels. Another 387 cars (1875-1978, 2001-2200) arrived in 1942-1943; again similar but with steel replacing wood for below-body toolboxes.

Santa Fe then turned to its own shops for its next cars, 200 in 1949 (500-599, 2201-2300). Their appearance was similar to the AC&F cars, but had peaked panel roofs, steel running boards, and taller (42-inch) end railings. The 2201-series cars had Duryea cushion underframes. Through the 1950s many of these and earlier cars were equipped with radio; to indicate this, an R was added near the road number.

An interesting detail on many Santa Fe cabooses starting in the 1930s days was the "wig wag" or "highballer," a round sign on a pivoting post mounted on each end of the

The Chicago & Eastern Illinois built 15 cabooses with angled, streamlined cupolas at its Oak Lawn shops in 1951. Number 7 is on a local freight switching at Brewer Yard in Danville, Ill., in December 1958. *J. Parker Lamb*

The Chicago, Burlington & Quincy built 25 conventional end-cupola steel cabooses at its Havelock, Neb., shops in 1930 as class NE-10 (nos. 13500-13524). They can be spotted by their radial roofs and single side cupola windows. They were painted in the railroad's maintenance-of-way orange scheme in the early 1950s. Number 13520 is at Sioux City, Iowa, in May 1970. *F. Hol Wagner Jr.*

The Burlington Route
built two series of
streamlined-cupola
waycars. Number 13537
is from the first series,
class NE-12, built in 1954.
The cupola ends were
at steeper angles on the
CB&Q cars compared to
the Wabash cabs; the Q
cars also only had a sin-
gle side cupola window.
This one, at Denver in
June 1968, is stenciled for
use on trains 71 and 72
only. *F. Hol Wagner Jr.*

Great Northern no. X310
was a one-of-a-kind
caboose built by the
railroad in 1955. It has
a welded body and a
rounded cupola with
contoured-side roof.
Also note the geared-rod
driven axle generator
(on the left axle of the
right truck) instead of the
more conventional belt
design. *Great Northern*

After the X310, the Great Northern redesigned the cupola with angled instead of rounded sides and ends. The resulting 30 stream-lined cupola cabooses (X1-X30) were built at GN's St. Cloud shops in 1958-1959. The shape of the cupola and windows is noticeably different compared to the Pennsy, Wabash, or Burlington cabooses. They made it to the BN roster as nos. 10361-10390. *GN Railway Historical Society Archives, Wade Stevenson Collection*

An Elgin, Joliet & Eastern caboose awaits its next assignment at North Chicago in March 1968. The steel caboose was built by International in 1956. It is riveted and features ICC's charac-teristic cupola style with peaked roof and shallow V-shaped end sills. It has electric markers on the end and a cupola-mounted marker as well (an EJ&E signature item). *Russ Porter; Don Heimburger collection*

cupola. Handles inside the cupola allowed crew members to move the device, signaling the head end. A light in the middle of the paddle allowed night operation. The faces of the paddles (and lights) faced the cupola, so it was the rear-most wig wag that was used to signal. Early versions had 18-inch-diameter disks painted blue with white centers; later versions were 29 inches across and painted yellow-orange; they were also perforated for wind resistance. Most were

removed by the mid-1950s as radio came into wide use.

The railroad began rebuilding these cars in the 1960s, reclassing them as they were rebuilt (each class of rebuilt cars included cars from several earlier series). The first 283 rebuilds, Cᴇ-1 (999000-999314), were done in 1966-1968. Work included stripping and replacing the interiors, rebuilding the trucks, sides, and roof, adding a Shock Control cushion underframe, adding new

Bessemer & Lake Erie painted caboose 1981 in red, white & blue to celebrate the nation's bicentennial in 1976. The former Elgin, Joliet & Eastern caboose was built by International in 1956. It has an offset cupola, riveted construction, and a shaft-style adapter for the generator mounted to an axle of the right-hand truck. It's shown here in June 1976. *Dennis Schmidt; Don Heimburger collection*

The Monon bought several steel cabooses from International in 1952 (nos. 81501-81509) with riveted bodies and slightly offset cupolas. Number 81506 is at Bloomington, Ind., in May 1971. *Dennis Schmidt; Don Heimburger collection*

sealed windows (locations and number vary), new generators and battery sets, and new numbers and bright red paint scheme. Rebuilding would continue through classes Cᴇ-2 (1969-1970), Cᴇ-3 (1968-1969, local service cars; yellow cupolas), Cᴇ-4 (three non-cupola cars for rotary dumper service (nos. 999637-999639), Cᴇ-5 (transfer service cars), Cᴇ-7 (local service), and finally Cᴇ-9 (in 1978).

Another Western railroad, Union Pacific, in 1942 began buying and building steel cars with a distinctive high-cupola design that would last through the 1980s. The first 100 cars were built by Mt. Vernon in 1942 (nos. 3700-3799) and became class CA-3, followed by 100 similar cars from Pullman-Standard in 1944 (CA-4; 3800-3899). They had riveted bodies and underframes, 30-foot bodies, and cupolas extending 4'-1" above the Murphy-panel roofs. They were delivered with wood-beam trucks; these were eventually swapped for outside- or inside-swing-hanger trucks as used on

The Norfolk & Western was a regular customer of International, owning more than 300 standard-cupola cabooses. Number 518525 is a class C-31P caboose built in 1969, one of 200 welded versions built from 1968-1970. It's shown here at South Yard in Roanoke, Va., in October 1995. *James Gillum collection*

Norfolk Southern restored former Norfolk & Western 555006 for use as a shoving platform. It's one of 100 welded cabooses built by International for N&W in 1976 (555000-555099). It's on a side track at Yuma, Va., in March 2017. *Malina McGee*

Great Northern caboose X76 trails a freight train from the Devil's Lake branch as it joins the main line heading east at Nolan, N.D., in July 1970 (making this a Burlington Northern scene). The caboose is one of 20 (nos. X66-X85) welded, standard-cupola cars built for GN by International in 1962-1963. *Russ Porter; Don Heimburger collection*

Detroit, Toledo & Ironton no. 110 is one of 18 riveted, standard-cupola cabooses built for the railroad by International in 1949. It's on a train at Sharonville, Ohio, in June 1976. It has a firecracker antenna on the cupola roof. *Dan Dover; Don Heimburger collection*

later cars. The UP then built the next three classes at its Omaha shops: 100 cars each in CA-5 (3900-3999), CA-6 (2700-2799), and CA-7 (25400-25499) in 1952, 1955, and 1959. These were similar, but had welded underframes, diagonal-panel roofs, and safety railings at the tops of the end ladders. The earlier cabooses were renumbered starting in 1959, to 25000-25399.

The railroad then turned to International Car Co. for its last three series of this design, 100 cars in classes CA-8 (1964, nos. 25500-25599) and CA-9 (1967, 25600-25699), and 50 cars in CA-10 (1975, 25700-25749).

These featured welded construction, and their wheelbase was 19½ inches longer than earlier cars. The CA-10 cars did not have running boards.

Many of these cars were upgraded for pool service starting in 1969, with new safety windows, retention toilets, electric service (axle-driven generators), and roller-bearing trucks (a large "P" on the sides and cupola indicated pool service). The CA-3s and -4s were delivered in red paint; the switch to yellow began in 1947. The CA-6 cars of 1955 were the first delivered with safety slogan frames. A few of the UP cupola cars wound

Peoria & Pekin Union no. 229 is a standard-cupola, welded caboose built by International. It's at Pekin, Ill., in September 1983. It was built with a running board, which has been removed; the top rung of the end ladder has also been removed. *Dennis Schmidt, Don Heimburger collection*

Grand Trunk Western no. 79059 is an end-cupola riveted caboose built by International in 1957. It's at Lansing, Mich., in July 1976. Screens now cover the windows and the running board and top rung of the end ladder have been removed. *Dennis Schmidt; Don Heimburger collection*

Chicago, Central & Pacific 199053 was built by International in 1970 for Gulf, Mobile & Ohio. It has the modern-style sealed cupola end windows with rounded corners. The CC&P acquired the caboose from Illinois Central Gulf. It's at Hawthorne Avenue Yard (Cicero, Ill.) in February 1991.
L. Regoli;
Don Heimburger collection

Seaboard Air Line bought 50 cabooses from International in 1949 (nos. 5600-5624) and another 50 in 1952 (5650-5699). The cars were 37 feet long over the end sills and 14'-8" to the peak of the cupola. The stacked windows on the right of the side are at the bunk locations. This is no. 5602's builder's photo from 1949.
International Car Co.

Boston & Maine C136, at White River Junction in July 1966, was built by International in 1959, but using underframes and trucks from retired B&M wood cabooses (4600-series) built by Laconia in 1921 (note the horizontal channel sill below the side). The 33-foot cars were originally numbered C100-C137; they were renumbered C51-C87 in 1975. *Robert Stonich collection*

Detroit & Toledo Shore Line no. 120 is a riveted conventional-cupola caboose built by International. It's shown here at Trenton, Mich., on Oct. 11, 1975. *Dennis Schmidt; Don Heimburger collection*

up on other railroads, including Montour; Pittsburgh & Lake Erie; and Utah Railway.

Another unique design belonged to the Illinois Central, which built more than 300 offset-cupola cars with small doors on each side. The first 100 came from the railroad's Centralia, Ill., shops in 1940, with another 100 in 1941 (nos. 9700-9899). The IC added another 64 in 1950-1951 (9918-9949, 9968-9999) and 50 in 1957-1958 (9600-9649). The cabooses have 28-foot bodies (33 feet over end sills), stand 14'-7" to the cupola top, and are riveted. The cupolas have slanted sides, with single windows on the sides and two front and back. Each side has four evenly spaced windows plus the small side door. Many remained in service through the Illinois Central Gulf merger (1972) and into the 1980s.

The New York, New Haven & Hartford in 1940 received the first 25 of what would become an iconic caboose design, the NE-5

Rio Grande began building steel cabooses to a standard design in its Burnham shops in 1940, turning out 70 riveted cabooses through 1951 (01400-01469) and another 21 welded cars in 1955 and 1959 (01470-01490). The cabooses had 29'-10" bodies with a tall end cupola. Number 01422 was built 1942 and is shown in September 1965. *Chris Burnitt; Don Heimburger collection*

Southern Pacific's most-common steel cupola caboose was the C-40-3 class, with 215 built from 1940-1942 (nos. 1050-1234 plus Texas & New Orleans 400-429). They were 36'-4" long with offset cupolas and peaked roofs. After these, SP turned to bay window cars. Number L1197 is at Gilroy, Calif., in June 1968. *Henry E. Bender Jr.; Don Heimburger collection*

class, built by Pullman-Standard. The cabooses followed a basic style common to railroads in the Northeast, with a short body (33'-8" over end sills; 18'-8" truck centers; 9'-6½" wide) and low-profile, centered cupola (13'-6" tall to top of cupola) with two windows on each side. It was one of the first cupola designs to feature welded construction, and had 14 low-profile vertical ribs on each side. The roof wrapped in a tight radius over the top of each side (the cupola roof also), giving it a distinct, easy-to-spot appearance. Another 50 cars followed in 1942 and 50 more in 1944 (nos. C510-C634).

The New Haven then turned to International Car Co. for its next cabooses, in 1947-1948: 75 cars in class NE-6 (C635-C709). These had a similar appearance to the NE-5s, but the sides had five panels, with four vertical seams. The cars also had panel-style roofs.

Along with the New Haven, Pullman-Standard built nearly identical cabooses to the NE-5s for Boston & Maine and Chicago Great Western. The 20 B&M cars were built in 1942 and 1944 (nos. C1-C10, C40-C49), and 25 CGW cars in 1945-46—the last cabooses built by P-S (nos. 600-624). (See page 15 in Chapter 1 for a view of a CGW

In 1941 Erie built 70 riveted cabooses at its Dunmore, Pa., shops (nos. C100-C169). The first of what became known as "Dunmore cabooses," they were distinctive for their short length; wide, straight-sided cupolas; express trucks (from retired milk cars); and window pattern (with drip rails). Number C118 is still running on successor Erie Lackawanna at Youngstown, Ohio, in July 1970. *Larry White; Dick Wallin collection*

Erie updated its Dunmore caboose design with welded construction, building another 100 in 1946 (C170-C269). The Dunmore design would be the railroad's signature caboose until the Erie-Lackawanna merger in 1960. Here mail and express are being loaded onto no. C190 at Woodville, Pa., in the early 1950s. The local freight will soon head to Shenango, Pa. *Erie*

caboose in its original scheme.)

The Chesapeake & Ohio bought its first steel cabooses in 1937, 50 built by Magor (nos. 90000-90049). They had a distinctive look: they were short (24-foot body; 32 feet over end sills) with slightly offset, angled-side cupolas and two windows on each side. Another 150 of the same basic design followed: 100 in 1941 (90050-90099 from Magor; 90100-90149 from St. Louis Car

Co.), and 50 from AC&F in 1947 (90150-90199). Similar cars were built for subsidiary Pere Marquette: 25 from Magor in 1937 (A901-A925), similar to the first C&O cars but on standard underframes (C&O's used Duryea cushion underframes). Another 40 came from St. Louis Car in 1941 (A950-A989); the difference included steel running boards and swapping the end ladder location from the right to left (as you look

Beginning in 1948, the Delaware, Lackawanna & Western's Keyser Valley shops built a series of steel cabooses atop old steam locomotive tender frames. The cabooses, nos. 850-910, had distinctive side sills, radial roofs, and four windows with inverted-V-shaped drip rails. Number C864 still wears Erie Lackawanna paint in November 1976, seven months after the Conrail merger. *Robert Stonich collection*

The Rock Island built 50 steel cabooses in 1930 (nos. 17850-17899). They had tall offset cupolas and five windows per side. Number 17853 is at Herington, Kan., in 1936. They would be rebuilt in the mid-1950s. *TRAINS magazine collection*

at the end. These all went to C&O when it merged PM in 1947.

The C&O bought a final batch of 150 standard-cupola cabooses in 1949: 100 for the Chesapeake District (90200-90299) and 50 for the PM district (former Pere Marquette lines; 90300-90349), which had ladders on the left side of each end. The C&O later rebuilt many cabooses from the 90000-90199 cars in 1969-1970, giving them new interiors and windows and renumbering them 3500-3684.

Streamlined designs

The Pennsylvania's N5c cars were the first cabooses to feature streamlined, multi-angle cupolas, and a few other railroads made forays into streamlined caboose design as well.

The Wabash had built 70 standard end-cupola steel cabooses in three series in 1939, 1941, and 1944 at its Decatur, Ill., shops (nos. 2700-2769). In 1945, the railroad followed with 20 cabooses (2770-2789) that had a tall, streamlined cupola (sides angled

The Great Northern built no. X199 at its St. Cloud, Minn., shops in August 1941. It's an early example of a welded offset-cupola caboose, and 47 cars of the basic design would be built through 1951 (X199, X229, X250-294). *Great Northern*

Northern Pacific built several series of steel cupola cabooses at its Brainerd, Minn., shops. Burlington Northern 11406 (ex-NP 10062) is one of 50 welded cars built in 1954 (10050-10099). It has an offset cupola and 30-foot body (35'-8" over end sills). *Don Heimburger collection*

in; each half of the front and rear angled in). The Wabash followed with three more 20-caboose series, in 1947-1948, 1949, and 1952 (nos. 2790-2849), and then in 1955 went to International Car Co. for 10 more of the same design (2850-2859). These cabooses were 35'-3" over sill plates and 14'-8¾" tall to the top of the cupola roof.

These wore several Wabash schemes, starting with red; many were repainted in the red and white scheme starting in 1960. With the railroad's merger into Norfolk & Western in 1964, the streamlined-cupola cars became N&W class C18 and were renumbered by adding "56" to the Wabash numbers (562770-562859). Many continued in service into the 1980s.

At the time these cars were being built, the Ann Arbor (which was under Wabash control at the time) received 17 cars of the same design. The only difference on these (nos. 2830-2846) was that they had steel end doors, while the Wabash cabs had wood doors.

The Chicago & Eastern Illinois followed suit, building 15 similar riveted cabooses

(nos. 7-21) at its Oak Lawn shops in Danville, Ill., in 1951. North of the border, Canadian Pacific in 1953-1954 built 50 long (40-foot) cabooses with centered, low-profile angled cupolas.

The Chicago, Burlington & Quincy was next. The railroad had built its first 25 steel cars, standard designs with an end cupola, as class NE-10 in 1930. The railroad then went 24 years without a new caboose, but in

If Spokane, Portland & Seattle no. 884 looks similar to the Northern Pacific caboose on page 91, it's because it was built by parent NP's Brainerd shops in 1954 as well, and differs only in minor details (window arrangement). The welded steel caboose has been freshly painted in this February 1962 view. *Merk Hobson*

Atlantic Coast Line's distinctive class M-5 cabooses were built from old 36-foot boxcars starting in 1964, continuing through the Seaboard Coast Line merger of 1967, until 1969 (nos. 0600-1036). They have 32-foot bodies (38 feet over end sills), 10 vertical riveted seams on each side, and angled-side cupolas. Number 0601 was just five months old when photographed in April 1965. *Wiley M. Bryan*

The Virginian had 50 steel cupola cabooses, including 25 of class C-10 (300-324) built by St. Louis Car Co. in 1949 and 25 of class C-10a, built by its Princeton, Va., shops in 1957 in 1957-1959, including no. 328. It has a coupled length of 34'-11". All went to Norfolk & Western in the 1959 merger. *Don Heimburger collection*

Norfolk & Western acquired a variety of caboose designs from other railroads through mergers. Number 557704 was built by Wheeling & Lake Erie in 1949, then almost immediately went to Nickel Plate in a merger, then to N&W in a 1964 merger. The series, 557700-557760, became class C-8 on the N&W. *James Gillum; N&W Historical Society collection*

1954 its Havelock, Neb., shops turned out 35 cabooses with tall streamlined cupolas. Numbered 13525-13559, they were railroad class NE-12. At first glance they resemble the Wabash cars, but the Q cars have taller cupolas with steeper angles on the end walls; the CB&Q cupolas also have only one side cupola window, and the bodies have a different window pattern. Havelock turned out 30 additional cars in 1960 (NE-12A; 13560-13589). These cars went to Burlington

Northern in the 1970 merger (renumbered 10391-10425 and 10331-10360), with many running into the 1980s.

Great Northern experimented with a streamlined design in 1955 when its St. Cloud (Minn.) shops turned out no. X310, a one-of-a kind caboose with a rounded cupola design. The 30-foot-body car remained unique and wasn't repeated, but in 1958-1959 the GN revised the design and built 30 cars with slant-walled offset cupolas

Texas & Pacific built cabooses 2500-2593 from 1949-1955. They were riveted with panel roofs and measured 35'-10" long over end sills (28-foot bodies). The cupola, placed near the end, had a distinctively large side window opening with a pair of sliding windows in the opening. *Robert Stonich collection*

Chicago & Illinois Midland bought several cabooses from American Car & Foundry in 1937. They are 37'-9" long overall, with three vertical batten strips and several horizontal rivet lines, a unique window style and arrangement, and centered cupolas with slightly angled sides. Number 70 is at Springfield, Ill., in December 1970. *Don Heimburger collection*

(X1-X30). The 32-foot cars had a stocky appearance, with a steeply slanted cupola. They also went to BN in the merger, and were renumbered 10361-10390.

International Car Co.

Through the 1940s, as steel cabooses became the dominant style, many railroads continued building their own cars. Several traditional freight-car and passenger-car builders (AC&F, Pullman-Standard, St. Louis Car Co., Magor, and others) also built cars, either to designs of their own or of railroads. One company began to emerge as a specialty caboose builder: International Car Co.,

which had offices in Buffalo, N.Y., and its manufacturing plant in Kenton, Ohio.

The company would become best known in the mid-1950s and later for its line of standard bay window and wide-cupola cars (which are covered in detail in Chapter 5). However, starting around 1941, ICC built hundreds of standard-cupola cars for many railroads, including Akron, Canton & Youngstown; Bessemer & Lake Erie; Boston & Maine; Chicago & Eastern Illinois; Detroit, Toledo & Ironton; Elgin, Joliet & Eastern; Grand Trunk Western; Great Northern; Gulf, Mobile & Ohio; Monon; Norfolk & Western; Northern Pacific;

Wabash; and others. Many other railroads acquired these cabooses second-hand through mergers or sales.

Although overall styles varied—including size, cupola placement, and window placement—the use of standard components made these cabooses recognizable and identifiable. Common attributes of International cabooses include a peaked panel roof, cupolas with peaked roofs and two side windows with an angled overhang above them (with sealed windows in two sizes; square corners early, and rounded corners on later cars), and car frames with end sills having a distinctive shallow V angle. Many earlier ICC cabooses are riveted; by the late 1950s, welded construction was more common.

Canadian Pacific no. 437498 is a steel center-cupola caboose, one of 100 built in 1953-1954. It's 33'-2" long over end sills. It's at Moose Jaw, Sask., in August 1968. *Robert Stonich collection*

Canadian Pacific had more than 130 steel cabooses with tall end cupolas. They were originally numbered in the 437000s when built in 1948, and many were eventually rebuilt and modernized and renumbered into the 434000s. Number 434026 has been modernized and repainted in CP's multimark scheme in this late 1970s view. *Russ Porter; Don Heimburger collection*

Ferrocarril Sonora-Baja California no. 4906 is a riveted caboose with a tall, centered cupola and express trucks. The railroad extended from a Southern Pacific interchange at Calexico, Calif., southward to the Ferrocarril del Pacifico in Benjamin Hill, Sonora. This caboose was built in 1960; it's shown in October 1966. *Henry E. Bender Jr.; Don Heimburger collection*

Other steel cars

Many other railroads built and bought cabooses in dozens of styles and variations from the 1940s through the 1970s. Some were built new from the ground up; railroads and builders often used frames from older equipment (cabooses as well as various freight cars) as the starting point. Although some railroads stuck with the same basic design for decades (such as Santa Fe and Union Pacific), many others built small batches of cabooses to varying designs as they needed them.

By the late 1960s, mergers were happening at an increasing rate. These new large railroads acquired a wide variety of rolling stock, including cabooses, from multiple predecessor railroads. Some were quick to repaint and renumber inherited cars; others could be found still rolling in their original schemes for years.

The many short lines and regional railroads that started operations in the 1970s and later often purchased second-hand cabooses from a variety of sources.

Bay window and wide-cupola cars became increasingly common by the 1960s and 1970s—more on those in Chapter 5—with fewer standard-cupola cars being built. The overall decline in caboose construction and ownership would continue through the 1980s, as explained in Chapter 8.

Radio systems

Shortly after the end of World War II, most U.S. railroads had various forms of radio-telephone communications under testing or in preliminary use. For the first time, the engineer and conductor could converse from their respective stations at each end of the train. Either could individually contact the dispatcher as well. Because the early vacuum tube-powered VHF equipment was bulky and heavy, it had to be mounted in place. That generally limited telephone handsets to the caboose and locomotive. The words "Radio-Equipped," frequently with stylized lightning bolts at each end, were applied to thousands of locomotives and cabooses from the late 1940s through the 1950s.

A particularly distinctive early railroad radio system was introduced in 1947 when the Pennsy began installing its train-phone system. Technically it was an inductive system rather than radio, essentially using the rails and lineside wires as antennas to transmit. The antenna looked like a handrail with stanchions mounted on caboose and locomotive roofs alike.

Most other railroads began using standard radio systems as technology became more widely available in the 1950s. Along with lettering, cabooses carrying radios could be identified by their rooftop (or cupola-rooftop) antennas. These were various styles; around 1950 the Southern Pacific introduced its system, which included an antenna that resembled an oversized roof-mounted horizontal brakewheel atop a post (made by Bendix). The Burlington also used a similar system. Other common antennas were the "firecracker," made by Motorola, which had a cylinder atop a thin post (looking like an inverted firecracker); whip, with a long metal rod; "can," which looked like a coffee can; and Sinclair, a low-mounted blade-shaped metal plate.

Early radio systems involved a lot of heavy, bulky equipment, as on this 1950s Missouri Pacific installation. The large black cabinets on the left hold separate electronics for cab-to-caboose and caboose-to-station communications, with separate handsets mounted near the cupola steps. *Missouri Pacific*

Chapter 4

The 'North

READING'S ADAPTATION OF THE USRA DESIGN BECAME A POPULAR, ICONIC CAR

Reading pioneered what became known as the "Northeastern" caboose in 1924, based on the earlier USRA wood design. Characteristics include steel body, sloped-side cupola, and paired windows on the ends of each side. The design would be copied by several other railroads. Number 92882 is a member of class NML, built in 1941. This class was similar to earlier cars, but with cast trucks and AB brakes. *Reading Co.*

eastern'
caboose

WATCH YOUR STEP

Reading 92850 is a class NMj car, built in 1936. It has the two inner windows plated over (a common late modification) and it wears the railroad's late yellow and green scheme in this view from July 1975 at Tamaqua, Pa. *Dennis Schmidt collection*

In 1924 the Reading Company embarked on a program of augmenting and replacing its aging wooden caboose fleet with new all-steel cars. This would simultaneously reduce maintenance on the cars themselves and allow the use of large, articulated steam locomotives in pusher service without the time and effort required to switch wood-framed cabooses behind the pusher (to avoid reducing them to kindling!) and back. Reading's design would soon became popular with other railroads, and versions of these cars would continue rolling through the coming of diesel locomotives all the way to the end of the caboose era in the 1980s.

Reading was pleased enough with its design to keep building them (with minor modifications) through 1948, and following the success of the Reading's original cabooses, five other railroads—starting with the Western Maryland—built their own versions (or contracted with Reading to build them) beginning in 1936. By 1948, more than 600 of what became informally known as the "Northeastern caboose" were operating on railroads along the Atlantic seaboard.

What eventually helped make these cars extremely popular among railfans and modelers was their rather amazing lineage, as hundreds eventually found homes with second-hand owners through sales and mergers. As route-miles and traffic declined on original owning railroads through the 1960s, these lines sold off many of them to more than 30 other railroads across the country—including short lines as well as many major railroads definitely not in the Northeast, such as the Chicago & North Western; Belt Railway of Chicago; Rock Island; and many others. In addition, mergers brought them to other major lines, including Conrail; Norfolk & Western; and Chessie System.

Let's start with a look at the original

design, and see how the cabooses evolved over the years.

Reading

The Reading Company's new caboose was based on the United States Railroad Adminisration (USRA) design of 1919 (see "USRA Cabooses" on page 107), but the Reading upgraded it to an all-steel car, substituting steel side sheathing and roof for the USRA-recommended wood. The Reading built the first 10 of these cabooses in 1924, and they become railroad class NMᴅ. Coupled length was 34'-11½" (the body itself was 25 feet long), while length over the running board was 32 feet. The body height

The class NMɴ cars, built in September 1942 when steel was in short supply because of World War II, had wood sheathing but steel framing and underframe. Body style and window placement remained the same as the steel cars.
M.D. McCarter collection

Class NMᴏ caboose 94002, at Allentown, Pa., in November 1966, was built by Reading in June 1943. The class returned to steel sides following the wood sheathing of the 1942 cars. Electric marker lights have been added at all corners.
J.W. Hulsman

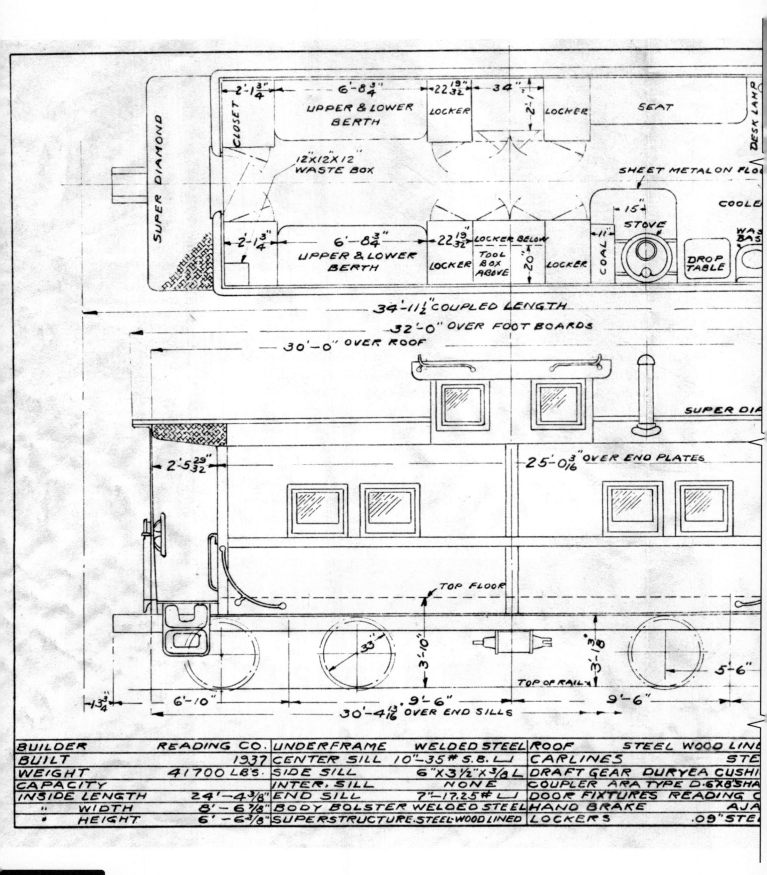

BUILDER	READING CO.	UNDERFRAME	WELDED STEEL	ROOF	STEEL WOOD LINE
BUILT	1937	CENTER SILL	10"-35# S.B. ⌣	CARLINES	STE
WEIGHT	41700 LBS.	SIDE SILL	6"X3½"X⅜ L	DRAFT GEAR	DURYEA CUSHI
CAPACITY		INTER. SILL	NONE	COUPLER	ARA TYPE D·6"X8"SHA
INSIDE LENGTH	24'-4⅜"	END SILL	7"-17.25# ⌣	DOOR FIXTURES	READING C
" WIDTH	8'-6⅞"	BODY BOLSTER	WELDED STEEL	HAND BRAKE	AJA
" HEIGHT	6'-6⅜"	SUPERSTRUCTURE	STEEL·WOOD LINED	LOCKERS	.09" STE

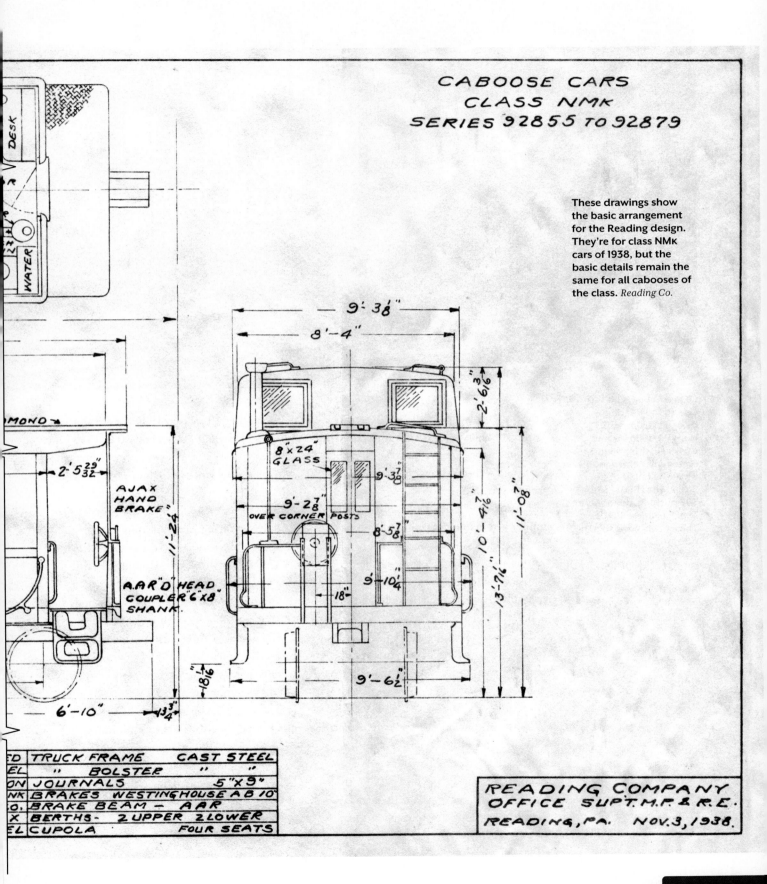

CABOOSE CARS
CLASS NMK
SERIES 92855 TO 92879

These drawings show the basic arrangement for the Reading design. They're for class NMK cars of 1938, but the basic details remain the same for all cabooses of the class. *Reading Co.*

DESK

WATER

DIAMOND

2'-5 29/32"

AJAX
HAND
BRAKE

11'-24"

A.A.R "D" HEAD
COUPLER 6"x8"
SHANK.

6'-10"

13 3/4"

18 1/16"

9'-3 1/8"
8'-4"

2'-6 3/16"

8"x 24"
GLASS

9'-3 7/8"

9'-2 7/8"
OVER CORNER POSTS

8'-5 7/8"

18"

9'-10 1/4"

9'-6 1/2"

10'-4 7/16"

11'-08"

13'-7 6"

FD	TRUCK FRAME	CAST STEEL
EL	" BOLSTER	" "
ON	JOURNALS	5"X9"
NK	BRAKES WESTINGHOUSE AB 10"	
O.	BRAKE BEAM - AAR	
X	BERTHS - 2 UPPER 2 LOWER	
EL	CUPOLA	FOUR SEATS

READING COMPANY
OFFICE SUPT. M.P. & R.E.
READING, PA. NOV. 3, 1938.

Lehigh Valley built 140 cars to the Reading design starting in 1937. Number 95064 is an early car with a single rectangular end window. It's at the tail of train BNE-2, with EMD F3 no. 502 pushing at Mountain Top, Pa., in the 1940s. The LV cars have angled drip strips above the windows. *W.R. Osborne*

to the top of the cupola was 13'-7¹⁄₁₆" (the coal stove smoke jack extended several inches above the cupola). The distinctive centered cupola had sloped sides with eight windows—two facing each direction.

The sides had a horizontal batten strip running just below the center of the car, and a vertical strip centered on the car side (starting just below the center of the cupola). Each side had a pair of rectangular windows placed toward each end, located directly atop the horizontal batten strip.

The cars were equipped with K brakes (standard for the time). The most dated feature on the cabooses were the trucks: archbar trucks with coil springs, salvaged from retired freight cars.

The interior included a coal stove with coal bin, wash basin, water cooler, desk with lamp, one bench seat, twin upper and lower berths, and closet and locker space (see the plans on pages 102-103). The cupola contained twin bench seats for four crewmen. Note that a toilet was absent!

Pleased with its new design, the Reading

built another 10 each in 1926 and 1927 (classes NMe and NMf) and 20 in 1930 (NMg). The 1930 cabooses were the first with cast-steel trucks (Taylor design), although the earlier archbar-equipped cabooses eventually received Taylor trucks as well. Even during the worsening Depression, Reading built another 20 cabooses in 1931-1932 (NMh), these with Commonwealth cast steel underframes.

As the Depression eased, Reading added another 25 cabooses each in 1936 and 1937 (classes NMj and NMk) followed by an additional 50 in 1941 (NMl). These were near-duplicates of their predecessors, but all were mounted on Duryea cushion underframes. This patented underframe had an internal shock absorber to minimize the jarring action of coupling and train slack running in and out—which was bad for freight, but especially dangerous for crewmen at the end of a long train. The underframe stretched the coupled length of the 1936 and later cars to 32'-8".

Another technical upgrade to these cars

was AB brakes, with Andrews leaf-spring trucks replacing the earlier Taylor design. The NML class was also the first appearance of metal running boards, replacing the wood planks of earlier cars. Another change was the elimination of below-body toolboxes, used through the NMj cars.

For the next batch of cars Reading modified the all-steel standard due to wartime restrictions on steel useage, building 50 composite cabooses in 1942 with wood-sheathed (steel-framed) bodies and wood roofs atop Duryea underframes (class NMn). The War Production Board loosened its restrictions in 1943, allowing Reading Shops to build 50 additional all-steel versions (NMo). The railroad built the final 25 cars to this design in 1948 (NMp), all on Duryea underframes, for a grand total of 295 Reading standard cabooses.

Lehigh Valley no. A95088 trails a piggyback flatcar on Norfolk & Western at Conneaut, Ohio, in July 1974. The "A" indicates a caboose in pool or run-through service. The car has been equipped with sliding screens in brackets over the side and cupola windows. *Don Heimburger collection*

Lehigh Valley numbered one of its Northeastern cabooses 1776 and painted it in red, white, and blue for the Bicentennial. It's at Chicago in August 1976. Note the fuel filler pipe (for the oil stove) on the right. *Robert Stonich collection*

Western Maryland built 105 cabooses from 1936 to 1940 at its Hagerstown, Md., shops following the Reading design. Note the lack of above-ladder grab irons on No. 1802 at Elkins, W. Va., in 1939. *John Vachon, Library of Congress*

Number 1881 wears Western Maryland's speed-lettering scheme at Baltimore in November 1961. It otherwise maintains its as-built appearance, including Andrews leaf-spring caboose trucks. *Bob's Photo*

Reading upgraded its cabooses over the years with the 1950s addition of radios and electric interior lights and markers (powered by an axle-driven generator) and flush toilets. Sealed windows and safety glass were installed during the 1960s, with the inner windows on the sides plated over. The original caboose red scheme gave way to green and yellow beginning in 1965, with all remaining cabooses repainted by the early 1970s.

The Reading cabooses served long service lives, with 119 still in service when the railroad became part of Conrail in 1976 and more than 100 still rolling in 1981. The wood-sheathed NMn versions were generally the first to be retired (they were off the roster by 1970), with the all-steel cabooses going to Conrail.

In addition, Reading had begun selling off many cabooses (especially older cars) from the late 1950s onward. These went to more than a dozen other railroads including Akron, Canton & Youngstown; Ashley, Drew & Northern; Belfast & Moosehead Lake; Belt Ry. of Chicago; Cedar Rapids & Iowa City; Elgin, Joliet & Eastern; Maryland & Pennsylvania; and Savannah & Atlanta.

Adopted by others

The industry (particularly neighboring railroads) quickly acknowledged the excellence of Reading's design and began building or ordering their own versions. The various railroads made individual modifications and improvements, including interior furnishings, window type, and trucks, but the lineage of all of them was unmistakable.

The Western Maryland in 1936 was the first to copy the Reading's cabooses. Similar cabooses were soon built by the Pittsburgh & West Virginia; Lehigh Valley; and Central Railroad of New Jersey; they eventually became generically referred to as the "Northeastern" design. Most were built by railroads' own shops; the Reading itself

Pittsburg & Shawmut no. 163 was built by American Car & Foundry following the USRA wood caboose design. It rides on Andrews leaf-spring trucks. Note the below-floor equipment box and the lack of curved grab irons above the end ladders.
American Car & Foundry

USRA cabooses

The United States Railroad Administration (USRA) took over operations of the nation's railroads in December 1917 in response to large-scale traffic congestion and shipping delays (especially across multi-railroad routings) at the onset of U.S. involvement during World War I. This control lasted until March 1920. During this time, the USRA developed several standard modern railroad car designs in addition to a range of standard steam locomotives. Many of these designs remained popular with builders and railroads long after USRA control ended.

Along with freight cars, the USRA developed and adopted an eight-wheel caboose design in December 1919. In an era of all-wood cabooses, it represented a modern design, with a steel frame to withstand forces of pusher locomotives as well as to better handle increased train sizes and speeds and provide more safety in the event of rear-end collisions. The USRA car had a centered cupola and wood-sheathed body over steel framing. The interior was also wood-sheathed, and specifications called for a wood (tarred canvas) roof. Four-wheel trucks with cast bolsters and sideframes were specified—a number of different truck designs were used by railroads, including archbar, Andrews, and Bettendorf AAR standard.

The USRA itself did not order any cars built to this design, but as with USRA freight car designs, the caboose drawings and designs were offered to manufacturers and railroads to meet contemporary requirements. Boston & Maine; Pittsburg & Shawmut; Ulster & Delaware; and Central Vermont were among the railroads that built cars to the basic USRA design (individual details were left to each railroad's determination).

Although the total number of USRA-design cabooses built was small, the design was a key in the development of the Northeastern caboose, as the Reading and other builders adopted steel sheathing and other improvements to create a distinctive, iconic design.—*Gordon Odegard*

served as a contractor, building five all-steel cars for Lehigh & New England in 1937 and eight composite-body cars for Lehigh & Hudson River in 1942, and supplying components for others.

Next to the Reading, the Lehigh Valley had the largest caboose fleet of the design, with 140 cars built from 1937 to 1946. They followed the same general lines as the Reading cars, with 94 equipped with Duryea cushion underframes and the rest with standard (non-cushioned) steel underframes. The LV applied angled drop rails above each pair of side windows, giving them a distinctive appearance.

The LV's initial 20 cars of 1937, built by the railroad's Sayre, Pa., shops from components supplied by Bethlehem, were based on Reading's NMj cars of 1936. Known as early Phase I cars, they had a single rectangular window on each end (to the extreme right when viewing the end from the outside) and ladder side rails that terminated at the roof (with separate curved grab irons extending above the roofline). They lacked the under-body toolboxes of the early Reading cars, but had Duryea underframes and rode on Birdsboro trucks.

Another 75 cars built by the LV from 1939 through 1944 were similar, but many received two rectangular end windows, and the ladder side rails continued upward to serve as hand holds (and they were a different shape than earlier cabooses). Other features remained the same.

Lehigh Valley's final 45 cabooses, built in 1945 and 1946, were known as Phase II designs. The most noticeable difference was a pair of round porthole-style windows on each end (instead of rectangular). These also had cast steps (earlier versions had fabricated steps), standard (non-cushion) underframes, and rode on Gould caboose trucks.

The LV cabooses wore many paint schemes, starting with a simple freight car red with the railroad name and "ROUTE OF

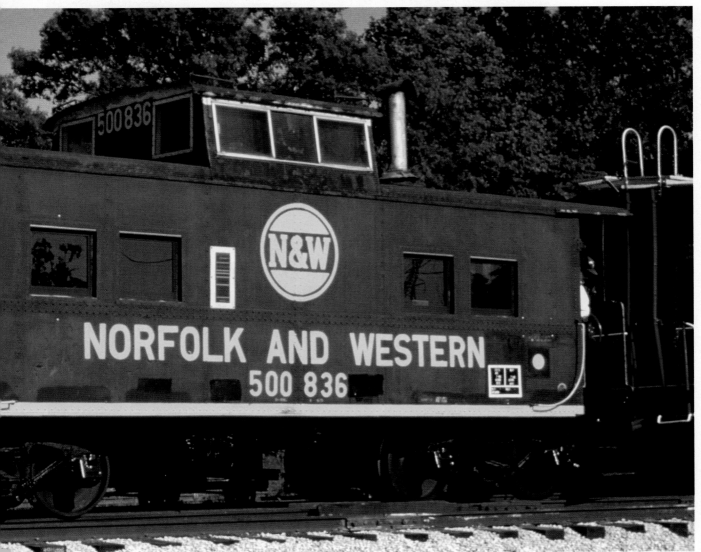

Lehigh & New England's five Northeastern cabooses were built by Reading in 1937. After retirement no. 580 was restored; it's part of the Tri-State Railway Historical Society collection in New Jersey.
Dick Wallin; Don Heimburger collection

Delaware & Hudson acquired Northeastern cabooses second-hand from Lehigh Valley. Number 35802 is ex-LV 95109, one of the railroad's later cars with round end windows.
Don Heimburger collection

Pittsburg & Shawmut bought second-hand Northeastern cars from both Reading and Lehigh Valley. Number 196 is a late ex-LV car (note the round end windows) painted red, white, and blue in September 1979 at Kittanning, Pa.
J. David Ingles

THE BLACK DIAMOND" slogan, but followed by multiple lettering and logo combinations on cars of various shades of red, Penn Central green, and white. Most cabooses were assigned to specific divisions; an "A" prefix to the car number indicated pool service.

A total of 92 LV cars survived to the Conrail merger in 1976. As with the Reading, the Lehigh Valley sold many of its cabooses to other railroads—including some major lines—from the 1960s into the 1970s, including Chicago & North Western; Delaware & Hudson; Detroit & Toledo Shore Line; Penn Central (which would wind up back with Conrail); Pittsburg & Shawmut; Providence & Worcester; Rock Island; and Toledo Terminal.

The Western Maryland was next in number of these cabooses, with 105 built from 1936 through 1940 (railroad class NE). The railroad's Hagerstown, Md., shops turned out its first 25 cars in 1936, using components supplied by Bethlehem Steel. Another 25 followed in 1937, plus 55 in 1940 (car nos. 1801-1905).

The WM cars followed the basic design of Reading's NMj cabooses of 1936, with Duryea underframes, but they lacked the under-body tool boxes of the Reading cars. The WM cars rode on a mix of Andrews, Birdsboro, and Gould caboose trucks. Later

Akron, Canton &
Youngstown no. 66 is a
former Reading caboose.
It's looking a bit worse
for wear, but still has its
original windows and
window arrangement at
Akron, Ohio, in July 1972.
Don Heimburger collection

body modifications included screens over the windows, sealed safety-glass windows, and plating over window openings.

Paint schemes included the railroad's original caboose red with circular logo, followed in 1955 by a boxcar red body with WESTERN MARYLAND spelled out in its then-new italic "speed lettering" scheme with striping. The last pure WM scheme was the red, white and black scheme that appeared in 1969.

As with other initial owners, the WM sold many of its Northeastern cabooses to other railroads starting in the 1960s. They went to Apalachicola Northern; Chesapeake & Ohio; Maine Central; South Branch Valley; and Tennessee Central. A handful went to the Gulf, Mobile & Ohio, rebuilt with new wide cupolas in place of the originals (see page 155). By the Chessie System merger of 1973, 69 of WM's Northeastern cabooses were still in service. Many kept rolling into the 1980s, having received the standard Chessie System scheme (with WM reporting marks), as well

as at least one oddball in blue (see page 114).

Next in numbers among original owners was Central of New Jersey, which built 50 cabooses (nos. 91500-91549) in 1942 from components supplied by Reading. These became CNJ class NE cabooses. The CNJ cars were quite similar to Reading's latest version (NML), and were all-steel with Duryea underframes and Andrews leaf-spring trucks. The CNJ cars had the same side window pattern as other Northeastern cars, but the railroad plated over the side window adjacent to the stove (look directly below the stack), so one side had only three windows.

The CNJ cars were painted caboose red with the railroad's Statue of Liberty logo, which changed to a bright red scheme in the 1970s. Unlike other original owners, CNJ kept its fleet largely intact; when CNJ became part of Conrail in 1976, 45 of the cars were still in service (although they had the reputation of being in rough shape by that point).

A trio of small railroads rounded out the list of original owners. The Pittsburgh &

West Virginia, a short bridge line operating from Connellsville, Pa., westward through Pittsburgh and through West Virginia and into Ohio, built 15 Northeastern cabooses from 1940 to 1944 (nos. 825-839, class C-19). The cars, built by the railroad's Rook Shops from components supplied by Bethlehem, were nearly identical to the Western Maryland cars. All but one had Duryea underframes; they rode on Barber-Bettendorf caboose trucks (with leaf springs).

The Norfolk & Western leased the P&WV (essentially absorbing it) in 1963, thus acquiring all 15 of the P&WV cars. They remained in operation on the N&W, usually staying in their original operating region, albeit painted in N&W's blue scheme. Most ran through the 1980s.

The Lehigh & Hudson River's eight Northeastern cars (class NE) were built by the Reading in 1942 as part of that railroad's NMn series. The composite cars have wood sheathing and roofs over steel framing and ride on Duryea cushion underframes, also riding on the same Birdsboro trucks used by that Reading class. As the wood sheathing aged, the L&HR eventually applied plywood sheathing to four of the cars. Six of the cabooses lasted until the formation of Conrail in 1976; their deteriorating wood bodies led to their retirement shortly thereafter.

The smallest original roster was that of the Lehigh & New England, with five cabooses. All (nos. 580-584) were built by Reading in 1937. They were near copies of Reading's NMk cabooses, with Duryea underframes, but on Barber-Bettendorf caboose trucks. They also had under-body tool boxes, which the Reading installed on its earlier cabooses but omitted on its NMk cars. The paint scheme was caboose red with the railroad's logo and number.

When the L&NE ceased operations in 1961, the Central of New Jersey took over operations on about 40 miles of former

Kalmbach Media

American Flyer icon

An additional boost to the popularity and recognition of the Northeastern caboose came via a toy company, the A. C. Gilbert Company of New Haven, Conn. In February 1938, Gilbert purchased The American Flyer Manufacturing Company of Chicago. Gilbert was a successful manufacturer of Erector sets, Mysto Magic sets, Polar Club brand small appliances, and fractional horsepower electric motors. With the purchase of American Flyer, Gilbert entered the toy train business and found itself competing against the entrenched leader, Lionel. Determined to build a distinctive line, between 1939 and 1941 Gilbert embarked on a program converting American Flyer trains to 3/16" (S) scale, from Lionel's 1/4" (O) scale or gauge.

World War II intervened, but in 1946 Gilbert's first S gauge trains running on two-rail track were introduced—with an excellent copy of the Reading standard all-steel caboose included in each freight train set. Over the next two decades, 3/16"-to-the-foot copies of Reading cabooses were made by the tens of thousands. They remain so common that even at train shows today they can be had for under $10.

The Flyer cabooses were offered in many variations: with or without lighting, plastic window-light diffusers, and roof ladders; some even had a little solenoid-controlled brakeman with a lantern who leaned off the rear platform when the train stopped.

A. C. Gilbert entered bankruptcy in 1966 and passed from the scene soon thereafter. The Reading Company lasted a few more years, but in 1976 its rail assets (but interestingly enough, not the Reading Shops), became part of Conrail, and the era of the Reading/Northeastern caboose entered twilight. The popularity (and abundance) of these models lingers on, and remains a reason why when many hear the word "caboose," their resulting mental image is of the Reading/Northeastern design.

Western Maryland no. 1811 has been painted in Chessie System blue (instead of the standard yellow) in this 1977 view at York, Pa. The window behind the stove has been plated over; other new sealed and sliding windows have been added, along with small permanent electric marker lights. *Glenn E. Dietz*

L&NE line around Bethlehem, Pa. (which had a lot of cement traffic). The CNJ acquired the L&NE's five Northeastern cabooses, three of which survived through the Conrail merger in 1976.

The Conrail merger gave that railroad a fascinating, eclectic mix of cabooses with histories dating back to more than a dozen railroads. This included 262 Northeastern-style cars from the Reading, LV, CNJ, and

L&NE. Many (other than the wood-bodied composite versions) remained in service well into the 1980s, albeit by then generally restricted to local service. Most were painted in Conrail's blue scheme within a couple years of the merger; some eventually received CR's light gray maintenance-of-way scheme.

Final years

As with any older cars, the Northeastern cabooses of the Reading and other railroads were modified over the years. Retention-type toilets (look for a rooftop vent) were installed in most by the 1960s, along with safety glass (often non-opening windows). Increased cases and severity of vandalism meant most windows were eventually either screened or plated over entirely, especially on cabooses that remained in the Northeast.

Electric lighting (interior and marker lights) became common by the 1950s—look for the axle-mounted pulleys that drove the generators. Oil heaters replaced older stoves (marked by a fuel filler pipe on the side wall—and often an accompanying fuel spill stain); refrigerators and water coolers

The Northeastern caboose finding a new home the farthest west is probably City of Prineville (Ore.) no. 201. The former Lehigh Valley car has round end windows and LV's familiar angled drip strips above the windows. The stove's silver fuel tank is centered below the body. It's at Prineville in September 1968. *Henry E. Bender Jr.; Don Heimburger collection*

Providence & Worcester no. 3001 is a former Lehigh Valley caboose built in 1942. It has a single rectangular end window and a fuel-oil filler pipe (for the stove) at the far right of the side. It's shown in January 1983. *Scott A. Hartley*

Another former Lehigh Valley caboose is Chicago & North Western 10804. Built in 1937, by the time of this 1973 photo at Chicago's Avondale Yard it had its cupola windows and two side windows plated over and was stenciled "**TERMINAL TRANSFER ONLY.**" *Bob Janz; C&NW Historical Society Archives*

The crew of Conrail's Ringtown (Pa.) local are on the rear platform of a former Lehigh Valley caboose as it approaches Lofty Tunnel in March 1981. The 18701 was one of 92 LV Northeastern cabooses to make it onto the Conrail roster.
Reuben S. Brouse; Brian Sopke collection

were also added. Radios became common by the 1950s, with rooftop antennae of various styles (and often "Radio Equipped" or similar side lettering and logos).

Another prominent visual change was the banning of rooftop running boards on freight cars in the mid to late 1960s. From about 1970 and later, running boards and end ladders were removed from cabooses. Platform railings were often extended (taller) with additional rails.

Reading's adaptation of the original USRA caboose proved to be a solid, long-lasting design. The substantial service lives and continued interest in the cabooses among railfans and modelers has made the Northeastern caboose an icon of railroading.

The conductor and brakeman of Western Maryland's Connellsville local freight enjoy the scenery and fresh air from the platform of Northeastern-style caboose 1802 in June 1952. The train is rolling around Helmstetter's Curve. *Robert Milner*

Chapter 5

Bay window & wide-cupola cabooses

Brand-new steel bay-window caboose no. 20306 carries the markers for a hot perishable train on New York Central at Garrison, N.Y., in 1952. The NYC staged the photo to show one of its 200 small-bay cabooses just built by St. Louis Car Co. The railroad would eventually acquire more than 400 bay window cars. *New York Central*

RAILROADS BEGAN
OPTING FOR THEM IN
LARGE NUMBERS FROM
THE 1950S ONWARD

Several railroads built their own bay window cars from older wood cabooses or boxcars. Chicago & Eastern Illinois no. 506, here at Brewer, Ill., in 1958, is one of 21 older boxcars rebuilt to cabooses from 1942-1944 at C&EI's Oak Lawn shops. The railroad opted for small window-only bays. *Henry E. Bender Jr. collection*

Railroad shop and operating personnel tend to be tinkerers, always looking for a better, more efficient way to do something. The bay window and wide-cupola cabooses are testimony to that: Both were solutions to problems of cupola crew safety, car clearance issues, and improving crew visibility of trains. They also brought in an era of standard designs for cabooses, allowing railroads to buy off-the-shelf models (albeit with many options and variations) rather than develop and build their own designs.

The Akron, Canton & Youngstown is credited with developing the idea of the bay window caboose in 1923, when it rebuilt 11 old wood boxcars into cabooses. The railroad's H.F. Grewe and J.M. Hood had the idea of extending bays outward from the sides, which was done on seven of the rebuilt cars. The off-center bays extended about 8 inches outward and had windows fore and aft (but not on the sides until they were later retrofitted).

Many other railroads would copy that idea with home-built, rebuilt, and modified wood cars through the 1940s and 1950s. In some cases the "bay" was a simple extension of a window opening outward; for others, the bays were car-height extensions from floor to roof (or nearly so).

Regardless of the specific design, the idea behind the bay window was improving caboose crew members' visibility over the side of the train ahead. Taller cars would sometimes block the forward view from a standard cupola, and it was difficult to get a good view of the train from standard side windows. Going outside to the rear platform to get a look was inconvenient, time consuming, and presented a safety issue, especially at night or in bad weather.

Bay windows eased vertical clearance issues, especially in the Northeast, which had lots of older, low-height tunnels and bridges, so railroads were severely limited in how tall a caboose cupola could be. Safety was improved, as slack action posed especially high risks for crew members in cupolas.

Top: In 1946 the Monon rebuilt 15 older wood cabooses, removing the cupolas and adding full-height bays with tapered ends and roof. They retained their top fascia boards. They were 36'-6" long over the end buffers. *M.D. McCarter; Don Heimburger collection*

Kansas City Southern in the 1940s rebuilt 20 single-sheathed boxcars into cabooses, adding full-height steel bay windows. The tall cars retained their Murphy steel ends and ride on conventional (coil spring) solid-bearing freight car trucks. *M.D. McCarter; Don Heimburger collection*

The Minneapolis & St. Louis began building wood bay window cars in 1942, turning out 56 cars through 1949. They had new wood bodies and steel frames, but reused other components from retired cabooses. Number 1133, built in 1945, is trailing a Chicago & North Western train in 1966. *Russ Porter; Don Heimburger collection*

Bay window development

The idea was therefore out there, but it was a pair of railroads—one Western line (the Milwaukee Road) and one Eastern road—(Baltimore & Ohio) that ran with the concept and created truly modern steel bay window designs.

In 1937 the Chicago, Milwaukee, St. Paul & Pacific's West Milwaukee Shops pulled several old wooden cabooses from the dead line, removed the cupolas, repaired the roofs, and added bay windows to the car sides. These bay windows were large, extending 12 to 18 inches outward from the car side, and stretched the full car height from floor to roof. A table and chairs (facing each direction) were placed inside the bay, enabling crewmen to view their train more easily and safely.

Convinced they had a winner, in 1939 the railroad applied the design to all-new steel cabooses. The West Milwaukee Shops had since 1934 been building welded steel passenger cars for its famous *Hiawatha* Chicago-Milwaukee-Twin Cities service.

The cars had distinctive horizontal ribs (stiffeners) on each side. Welded boxcars with horizontal ribs followed in 1937. The new cabooses followed those successful designs, using welded bodies with multiple horizontal external ribs, and bays centered on each side. Met-L-Wood components were used in the interiors, and the cars rode on passenger-style trucks, giving them a very smooth ride. These became the standard caboose on the railroad, and from 1939 to 1951 the Milwaukee Road built 315 rib-sided cabooses to similar style (although there were detail differences among individual batches of cars).

The Baltimore & Ohio had developed a similar program at roughly the same time to develop its own unique modern design. In 1936 the railroad's Mount Clare (Md.) shops removed the steel underframes from five damaged wooden cabooses. The frames were used through 1940 to construct five newly designed and very distinctive cabooses. Following the designs of the railroad's "wagon-top" boxcars, they had vertical steel

The "wagon-top" design was a Baltimore & Ohio trademark, with side sheets wrapping around the roof to the other side. Number C2502 was built in 1938 at the railroad's Mount Clare shops; it's on display at the New York World's Fair in 1939. *New York Central*

Milwaukee Road's welded rib-sided cabooses were revolutionary when introduced in the late 1930s, and the railroad would build more than 300 of them. Number 01892 has just been reconditioned and repainted in 1963. The panel under the window at left has the filler and fittings for the new oil heater. *Milwaukee Road*

International Car Co. became the major builder of bay window steel cabooses. Nickel Plate 400, built in 1952, is an early version featuring riveted construction. The interior (above right) has reversible bench seats at the bays. It still includes bunks: Two built in and two uppers that fold up when not in use. *Two photos: Nickel Plate Road*

Western Pacific favored bay window cabooses, having built several composite versions in the 1940s (see page 137). Welded bay window no. 430 is from the railroad's first order from International, 35 cars delivered in 1955-1956. It's at Klamath Falls, Ore., in July 1982. The shallow V-shaped angled end sills (painted red on this car) are an ICC spotting feature. *Robert Stonich collection*

side panels that curved tightly at the tops to form the horizontal roof, then arced another 90 degrees down to form the opposite side. The panels were butt-welded to create a seamless section, then riveted to external vertical steel ribs. A key element of the design was the lack of a cupola and addition of a bay window centered on each side.

These five experimental wagon-top cabooses were deemed successful, and a production run of 100 nearly identical cabooses followed (nos. C2400-C2499), built by the B&O's Keyser, W.Va. shops between December 1941 and January 1942. The cars had 24-foot bodies, were 32'-5" over strikers, and had Duryea cushion underframes and insulated, wood-lined interiors. Another 25

Caboose construction specifications

Even when caboose construction is "standardized," there are plenty of options and variations from railroad to railroad. Here's a typical set of specifications, in this case for a 200-car order for International wide-cupola cabooses by C&O: car nos. 3100-3199, ordered in 1967:

- Welded construction (except for some locations where riveting is required for increased strength or shear resistance).
- Cushioned underframe with a sliding center sill.
- Coupler pocket arrangement, couplers, and draft gear fittings from specific hardware suppliers.
- Body construction must minimize any corners or sharp edges in the interior.
- Platforms and steps are to be made with open self-cleaning grating.
- Safety glass is to be used in all window openings and mirrors.
- The entire car is to be lined with Met-L-Wood-type steel laminated sheets.
- Running boards are to be all steel galvanized open-type grating extending the length of the roof, exclusive of cupola.
- Three inches of fiberglass insulation is to be applied to the sides, ends, roof, and floor, with rigid Styrofoam substituted around all movable window sashes.
- Car is to be equipped with 50-ton swing-motion caboose trucks with roller bearings.
- Lettering and painting are to follow diagrams supplied by the railroad. Scotchlite lettering is to be applied where needed.

Most of the above specifications are relatively standard items found in cars built by International. Other optional items that can be installed include:

- Sliding sash windows in sides and end doors.
- Rock guard screens over windows.
- Steel toilet compartment with door, vent, safety handhold, and mirror.
- Stainless steel lavatory equipment.
- First-aid kit recessed into front panel of toilet compartment so it does not project into the interior.
- Seventy-gallon stainless steel water tank suspended from the ceiling.
- Water cooler/refrigerator.
- Cup dispenser and disposal receptacle.
- Fusee and torpedo rack.
- Conductor's desk with padded edges.
- Revolving high-backed seat for the conductor's corner desk.
- Walkover seats in the cupola.
- Oil heater with safety railing; 65-gallon oil storage tank.
- Electrical generating equipment and axle-mounted drive.
- Electric lighting and permanently mounted marker lights at each corner.
- Train radio equipment.
- Battery box, battery, and recharging receptacle.

A typical railroad's specification may take 15 typewritten pages, with some added pages of last-minute changes. Everything is carefully stated before an order is begun at the factory.

Source: C&O order specification memo to ICC

International built Erie C300 in January 1953. The riveted car has a tabbed side sill (tabs extend down from the sides, covering the ends of the bolsters and cross bearers) and rides on express-style trucks from old milk cars. *Erie*

were built in late 1945 (C2800-C2824). They became the railroad's class I-12, and most lasted well into the 1980s.

Since they would often be working in mountainous (pusher-locomotive) territory, they were equipped with long-handled extensions that allowed crewmen to close the angle cock on the train line from the platform, and also a chain that allowed pulling the car's uncoupling lever from the platform. Both were features that enabled pusher locomotives to be uncoupled "on the fly" without stopping the train (more on how that was done in Chapter 7).

The Milwaukee and B&O cars were popular with crews and management alike: Railroads found that bay window cabooses were simpler and less expensive to build than cupola designs; crewmen no longer had to climb internal ladders and risk being tossed down to the floor from the cupola seat by slack or derailments. The success

National of Mexico no. 44546 was built by International in 1975. The welded car has squared-off tabs on the side sill, rounded windows, and no running boards or end ladders.
M.D. McCarter; Don Heimburger collection

Delaware & Hudson bought eight new bay-window cabooses from International in 1968 (nos. 35720-35727). It also owned 13 former Erie and Erie Lackawanna cars built by ICC in 1953 and 1970 (35805-35817).
G.W. Hockaday; Don Heimburger collection

of the bay window concept on two major railroads helped influence other railroads and manufacturers to build and purchase them.

Modern bay windows

Although many manufacturers (including many individual railroads' shops) would build steel bay window cars, it was the International Car Co. (ICC) of Kenton, Ohio, that began building steel bay window cabooses to standardized, modular designs, and the company soon found customers among dozens of large and small railroads across the country. The company had been building cars since the 1920s and started specializing in cabooses in 1941, building conventional cupola cabooses and transfer cabooses as well as bay window and (later) wide-cupola cabooses for many railroads.

Among ICC customers for its bay window cabooses were Bessemer & Lake Erie; Burlington Northern; Chicago & Eastern Illinois; Chicago & North Western; Chicago Great Western; Erie; Green Bay & Western; Kansas City Southern; Long Island Rail Road; Milwaukee Road; Minneapolis, Northfield & Southern; Missouri Pacific; National of Mexico; Nickel Plate Road; Pecos Valley; Pittsburgh & Lake Erie; Southern Pacific; Union Pacific; and Western Pacific. Mergers led to these cars running on many other lines, including Conrail; Norfolk & Western; Soo Line; and Wisconsin Central.

Bay window cars built by ICC share a common basic appearance, but specific details vary by railroad, especially the shape of the bays (the slope of the roof of the bay), window locations and styles (sliding or fixed; square or rounded corners), and the side sill arrangement. Bodies measured about 31 feet long (cars were 36'-7" over end sills), but some shorter versions were built in the 1970s. The body width was 8'-7" and extreme width over the bays 10'-7".

The bay styles varied quite a bit. The bay

Far left: American Car & Foundry built Southern Pacific's first steel bay window cars in 1947. The riveted cars have bays that are shorter than the car sides, with tapers on the bay roof and base. Number 1263 is at Newman, Calif., in 1968. *Henry E. Bender Jr. collection*

Left: Fruit Growers Express built cars for several Eastern railroads. Chessie System (B&O) 904024 is a class C-27A car built by FGE in 1980; it's at Flint, Mich., in April 1987. The sides terminate above the straight side sill. Note the angled sliding screens over the sliding bay windows. *Dennis Schmidt collection*

Below left: Most of Southern's distinctive bay window cabooses were built by Gantt Manufacturing. They had prominent bays with tapered bay roofs, with large windows on each end of each side and another on the bay wall. Number X519, built in 1971, is at Irondale, Ala., in July 1988. *Jim Hediger*

Greenville built the NE-1 class of riveted steel bay window cabooses for Bessemer & Lake Erie in 1941. The 20 cabooses have distinctive off-center bays, and were the railroad's first steel cabooses. Number 1969 is at Branchton, Pa., in 1970. *Dennis Schmidt*

Milwaukee Road added to its steel bay window roster in 1956 with 100 cabooses from Thrall. The riveted cars had straight side sills, a riveted horizontal seam down the middle of the sides, and they rode on the same passenger-style trucks as the railroad's home-built cars. *Thrall*

roof on some cars sloped at a steeper angle than others, the bay at bottom was level on some cars and sloped upward on others, and later cars had wider bays than earlier cars. Among best ways to identify an ICC car is by the end sill (visible just below the platform): on ICC cars this has a shallow "V" shape.

Interior details allowed many options, some of which affect exterior details (such as stoves, toilet compartments, and radio equipment). By the time these cars were built, the era of living aboard a caboose on the road was passing; many (especially Eastern cabooses and those built in the 1960s and later) had limited (or no) bunks, instead providing extra built-in seats.

Most ICC cars were welded, but some early cars were riveted. They used diagonal-panel roofs into the 1970s, with X-panel design roofs starting in 1973. As with other cabooses, running boards and end ladders were eliminated around 1970, although some cars delivered after that continued to receive them.

In 1977, ICC became a division of Paccar (formerly Pacific Car & Foundry). The recession of the early 1980s greatly slowed orders; the company built its last cabooses (for NdeM) in 1982.

Other manufacturers of steel bay window cars included AC&F (Southern Pacific); Fruit Growers Express (Chessie System/C&O/B&O, Conrail, Family Lines, and Southern Ry.), Gantt (Southern), Greenville (B&LE, with offset bays), St. Louis Car Co. (New York Central), SIECO (Southern); Thrall (C&NW, CGW, GB&W, MILW),

The Georgia Railroad rebuilt several 1940s-era steel boxcars into bay window cabooses in 1970. Note how large no. 2867 is compared to the Louisville & Nashville bay window caboose ahead of it. *Don Heimburger collection*

Canadian Pacific had just three bay window vans: nos. 437265-437267, built at its Angus Shops in 1948. This one is at Calgary, Alberta, in July 1979. Note the roof-mounted fuel tank (for the oil heater) with amber warning light atop it. *Jim Hediger*

Florida East Coast was another railroad rebuilding steel boxcars into bay window cabooses. Number 803 is at New Smyrna Beach, Fla., in 1969; the railroad needed few cabooses at the time, as it was the first railroad to move to end-of-train devices. *Dennis Schmidt collection*

Southern Pacific built riveted bay window caboose no. 1332 in 1951. It is one of 50 in class C-30-6, the last cabooses built by SP and the last with solid-bearing trucks. It's at Santa Clara, Calif., in June 1968. *Henry E. Bender Jr.; Don Heimburger collection*

St. Louis-San Francisco no. 1726 is one of 10 bay window cabooses built by the railroad at its Consolidated Car Shops (West Shops) in 1979. The welded cars (nos. 1726-1735) have straight side sills, X-panel roofs, whip antennas, and lack end ladders and running boards. It is at Fort Worth in July 1980. *Bill Phillips; Don Heimburger collection*

Louisville & Nashville built 200 short (32'-7" over end sills) bay window cabooses at its South Louisville shops from 1963-1966. Originally numbered 1001-1199, they were later renumbered 6000-6199. Number 6168 has had side windows plated over and sports a fresh Family Lines paint scheme at DeCoursey, Ky., in June 1980. *Jim Hediger*

133

Bay window caboose no. 1432 is one of 200 built for Southern Pacific by Pacific Car & Foundry in 1961 (class C-40-4). These were Espee's last riveted cabooses. They featured a taller bay than earlier versions and they rode on roller-bearing trucks. They debuted the two-light "frog-eye" rooftop marker lights. Here a brakeman gives a highball to the head end of a sugar beet train in the Imperial Valley in 1961. *Don Sims*

and Whitehead & Kales (SP).

Some individual railroads also built steel cars, including Canadian Pacific; Florida East Coast (rebuilt from boxcars), Louisville & Nashville; Minneapolis, Northfield & Southern; Missouri-Kansas-Texas; New York Central (also for then-subsidiary Pittsburgh & Lake Erie); St. Louis-San Francisco; Southern Ry.; and Southern Pacific.

Southern Pacific operated the largest fleet of bay-window cabooses—all steel—with 891 bought and built from 1947 to 1980.

The first were 35 riveted cars built by AC&F in 1947 (class C-30-4, nos. 1235-1269), followed by 50 more built by the railroad from AC&F-supplied components in 1949 (C-30-5, 1270-1319). The SP built another 50 in 1951 (C-30-6, 1320-1369). The next came in 1961: 200 cars from Pacific Car & Foundry to form the largest bay-window class, C-40-4 (nos. 1400-1599). These had taller bays than the earlier cars. The SP went to Whitehead & Kales for its next 100 cars (C-40-5, 1600-1699), in 1963-1964.

The Southern installed solar panels (on the roof at left) on 40 of its 200-series local cabooses in 1979 (the yellow bay signifies a car in local service. The distinctive bay window car was built by Gantt as part of series 200-250 in 1971. *Jim Wrinn*

In 1946 the Chicago & North Western rebuilt an older wood cupola caboose into wood bay window car no. 11538. The railroad's first steel bay window cars were still seven years away. *Chicago & North Western*

Chicago & North Western no. 11125 is one of 50 built by International in 1966. It has had its end ladder and running board removed and a side window (on the left) plated over, and it's sporting a fresh paint job at Green Bay, Wis., in December 1981. Note the blue-painted axle-driven mechanism for the generator on the left truck. *Jim Hediger*

International built C3003 for Baltimore & Ohio in 1966 as one of 46 class I-18 cabooses (later Chessie class C24). Many railroads by the 1970s were painting cabooses with various safety slogans; Chessie System painted this car white with purple slogan and blue road name in 1973. *Chessie System*

New York Central painted this caboose with a safety slogan and lettering in 1957. Number 20207 is from the first production series of steel bay window cars on the railroad, one of 95 built by Despatch Shops in 1949. *New York Central*

The SP's early cabooses had bodies 8'-10" wide; 10'-10" over the bays. The bays did not extend all the way to the top of the car; the tops and bottoms of the bays were beveled. There were four rectangular windows on each side, plus sliding windows on the side of each bay and vertical windows on the end of each bay.

Beginning in 1965, SP turned to ICC for its remaining caboose orders, all of which were welded: 50 in 1965-66 (C-40-6), 50 in 1966-67 (C-40-7, with fewer windows), nos. 1700-1799. The next cars, 75 in 1970 (C-50-3), 55 in 1972 (C-50-4), and 51 in 1974 (C-50-5), nos. 1800-1980, were delivered without running boards. Earlier cars began having them removed as well. These also had narrower bays.

The SP's final three orders were also from International, but after it became a division of Paccar: 50 in 1978 (C-50-7), with single marker lights replacing the earlier twin "frog-eye" lights; 50 in 1979 (C-50-8), with X-panel roofs; and 75 in 1980 (C-50-9), with no side windows (nos. 4600-4774).

The Southern Railway had the next-largest bay window fleet, with 618 cabooses. The railroad built its first 48 steel cars in 1941-42 (nos. X2882-X2929). They proved popular, and the railroad built another 238 cars in three batches from 1948 to 1951. Southern turned to outside manufacturers after that, with three from SIECO in 1969, followed by several orders from Gantt Manufacturing of Greenville, S.C.: 316 cars from 1969 to 1977. Numbers X327-X592 and X600-X793 were road cabooses and wore the standard bright red scheme; nos. X200-X250 and X260-X271 were classified as local cabooses and had their bays painted yellow (and were sometimes nicknamed "yellow bellies"). Southern's final cabooses came from Fruit Growers Express, 12 bay window cars built in 1980 (nos. X315-X326).

Southern's modern bay window cabooses had a distinctive appearance, with single square windows at the end of each side, a single window centered on each bay wall, and a window (with windshield wiper) on each angled bay end. This end was wider than many other bay designs.

The Chicago & North Western was an early user of bay window cabooses, rebuilding several older wood cabooses with bay windows in the 1940s; subsidiary Chicago, St. Paul, Minneapolis & Omaha (Omaha

Western Pacific built 61 composite-side cabooses from old Pullman-Standard single-sheathed boxcars from 1942 to 1945. Number 645, one of 25 built in 1943, rests at San Jose, Calif., in March 1967. *Henry E. Bender Jr.; Don Heimburger collection*

The only cabooses bought new by Conrail were the 113 class N21 cars (nos. 21201-21313), built by Fruit Growers Express in 1980. Number 21313 has been freshly painted at Norfolk Southern's Juniata (Altoona) Shops in April 2014. *Don Wood*

Road) had similar cabooses. The C&NW bought its first steel bay window cars in 1953, acquiring 89 cars from International through 1956. The railroad went to Thrall for its next cars, 50 in 1959 (nos. 10900-11049), then went back to ICC in 1964 and 1965, buying 52 more; then followed with another 117 from ICC in four orders through 1974.

The North Western also acquired some cars second-hand, getting 15 in 1968 when it merged the Chicago Great Western: 10 built by ICC (10524-10533) and five Thrall cars (10534-10538). It also bought eight former Rock Island cars (11211-11218) after that railroad went bankrupt in 1980.

As the C&NW rebuilt these cabooses in the 1970s, all windows (except those on the bays) were plated over.

The New York Central was a major user of bay-window cabooses, preferring an abbreviated bay that was only as tall as the windows, with a bay roof that sloped from the side down to the bay wall. The railroad's Despatch Shops built three prototypes in 1948 (nos. 20200-20202), then followed with 100 production cars in 1949 (20203-20297 and 20498-20502, which were originally assigned to subsidiary Boston & Albany as B&A 1300-1304).

The railroad followed with an order of 200 nearly identical cars, this time built by St. Louis Car Co. in 1952 (20298-20497). Despatch Shops would add another 100 in 1963 (21000-21999); another four cars would come from subsidiary Peoria & Eastern, built by International in 1965 (P&E

Conrail acquired a substantial fleet of bay window cars from its predecessors. Number 24019, here at Flat Rock, Mich., on the Detroit, Toledo & Ironton in 1977, is one of 50 (nos. 2400-24049) built for Penn Central at Altoona Shops in 1969. The class N10 cars have New York Central-style bays and a mix of sealed and sliding windows. *Jim Hediger*

Grimy Rock Island 17093 is at Southern Pacific's Austin, Texas, yard in October 1979. Built by International in 1970, it's one of 127 cabooses owned by Union Pacific and leased to RI. It has had its running boards removed, as well as the top end-ladder rung. *Andy Sperandeo*

Darby built 42 stainless-steel cabooses for Kansas City Southern in 1964 and 1970 (nos. 302-344). Their finish was eye catching, as were their distinctive (and uncommon) Rockwell high-speed trucks. Number 321 is at Shreveport, La., in February 1977. *Jim Hediger*

Missouri Pacific built 100 new road cabooses that resembled transfer cabs, but with bay windows and roller-bearing caboose trucks. The simplified design was efficient and less expensive than a standard bay window or extended-cupola car. New no. 13719 rolls on a freight in October 1977. *J. David Ingles*

International built 100 class CA-11 cabooses for Union Pacific in 1979, the railroad's first new steel bay window cars (and final caboose order). Number 25855 is at East Los Angeles in February 1980. The cars had short bodies with large end platforms. Although they looked like transfer cabooses they were mainline-service cars. *Jim Hediger*

21496-21499). Another 10 cars were built by subsidiary Pittsburgh & Lake Erie at its McKees Rocks (Pa.) shops in 1950 (P&LE 500-509).

The Central modernized its cars in the 1960s, giving them generators and batteries, oil heaters (replacing coal), drip strips above the bays, and windshield wipers on the bay end windows. Most survived the Penn Central merger (1968) and eventually served Conrail (1976).

The Milwaukee Road supplanted its original fleet of 315 home-built welded rib-side cars with 100 riveted bay window cars from Thrall in 1956 (nos. 02115-02214), then added 15 more welded cars from International in 1973 (992215-992229).

Baltimore & Ohio continued adding bay window cabooses to its roster after its initial wagon-top cars. There were 111 plywood-side cars (classes C-17 and C-19, nos. C1800-C1835 and C2300-C2374), followed by 46 conventional-design steel cars from International in 1965-1966 (nos. C3000-C3045). Cars built and delivered in the Chessie System era include 225 class C-26 (C3700-C3827) and C-26A (C3828-C3924) cars from ICC starting in 1971, and then 222 class C-27 (nos. C3925-C3986) and C-27A (B&O 904000-904093, C&O 904094-904159) cars from Fruit Growers Express in 1978 and 1980.

Western Pacific was known for favoring bay window cabooses, eventually acquiring 122 wood and steel cars. The railroad began building composite-side bay window cars in 1942, rebuilding them from early single-sheathed boxcars. The WP built 62 of them

International delivered its first production wide-cupola caboose to Duluth, Missabe & Iron Range in 1952. It had a riveted body and square-corner windows. It established the basic appearance the company's cars would retain through the 1970s. *International Car Co.*

Wide-cupola owners

This list shows the original buyers of International Car Co. wide-cupola cabooses. Many passed all or some cabooses to secondary railroads through mergers or sales; these are shown in parentheses.

Atchison, Topeka & Santa Fe (Toledo, Peoria & Western)
Burlington Northern (Montana Rail Link)
Central Vermont
Chesapeake & Ohio (Chessie System)
Chicago & Illinois Midland
Chicago, Burlington & Quincy (BN)
Chicago, Rock Island & Pacific (Union Pacific; Chicago & North Western)
Colorado & Southern (BN)
Delaware & Hudson
Denver & Rio Grande Western
Detroit, Toledo & Ironton
Duluth, Missabe & Iron Range
Detroit & Toledo Shore Line (Grand Trunk Western)
Fort Worth & Denver (BN)
Grand Trunk Western (Duluth, Winnipeg & Pacific)
Great Northern (BN)
Gulf, Mobile & Ohio (Illinois Central Gulf; Chicago, Central & Pacific)
Indiana Harbor Belt
Maine Central
Milwaukee Road (Soo Line)
Missouri-Kansas-Texas (Union Pacific)
Missouri Pacific
National of Mexico
Nevada Northern
Northern Pacific (BN)
Reading (Conrail; Delaware & Hudson)
Richmond, Fredericksburg & Potomac
Rutland (D&H)
St. Louis-San Francisco (BN)
St. Louis Southwestern
Seaboard Air Line (Seaboard Coast Line; Seaboard System)
Soo Line
Spokane, Portland & Seattle (BN)

Non-ICC wide-cupola cabooses were operated by these railroads (note that several railroads owned both ICC and non-ICC versions)

Algoma Central
Canadian National
Canadian Pacific
Gulf, Mobile & Ohio (ICG, CC&P)
Illinois Central (ICG)
Missouri-Kansas-Texas (UP)
Monon (L&N)
Ontario Northland
Pacific Great Eastern (BC Rail)
St. Louis-San Francisco (BN)
Toronto, Hamilton & Buffalo

Sources: ICC records; Jim Eager roster, October 1995 RailModel Journal

through 1945, featuring single-sheathed construction (external steel framing with horizontal wood sheathing inside the framing).

The WP bought its first new steel bay window cars in 1955-1956, an order of 35 (426-460) from International. The railroad returned to ICC for 15 more in 1973-1974 (461-480), then bought its final cabooses from ICC in 1980 after it became a Paccar subsidiary: six cars (481-486) as part of SP's order for C-50-9 class cars.

Conrail became a major owner of bay window cabooses upon its formation in 1976, with more than 500 on its roster at one time. Most were inherited, including former NYC cars (273 of them), along with 100 cars built for Penn Central (50 by Altoona Shops and 50 from International) and a handful from Erie and Erie Lackawanna. Conrail also purchased one batch of cabooses new: 113 cars from Fruit Growers Express in 1978 (nos. 21201-21313).

A few other bay window cabooses warrant mention. The Rock Island acquired 130 steel bay window cabooses from International from 1967-1971 (nos. 17082-17211). Although wearing RI paint, the cabooses were actually owned by Union Pacific and leased to Rock Island, a financing arrangement based on UP's intended merger of RI—which was eventually denied by the Interstate Commerce Commission. The cabooses went to UP when RI discontinued operations in 1980.

Another interesting batch of cabooses were the stainless-steel cars built by Darby for Kansas City Southern. These 42 cars (nos. 302-344), built from 1964 to 1970, were easily spotted by their natural stainless finish. They rode on Rockwell high-speed trucks, another distinctive spotting feature (these trucks were also used on the final 10 ICC cabooses built for Rock Island).

By the late 1970s, caboose deliveries were becoming rare. Railroads that were

Among the earliest attempts at extending the cupola width was by Chicago Great Western, which rebuilt several old wood cabooses. Number 82 was built by Haskell & Barker in the 1890s and rebuilt in the 1930s. *TRAINS magazine collection*

The Monon gets credit for being the first to apply the extended-cupola idea to a modern steel caboose, with Thrall delivering production models starting in 1951. The Monon's version had a wide cupola, but it did not extend below the roof line. Number 81531 is at Hammond, Ind., in 1970. *Dennis Schmidt; Don Heimburger collection*

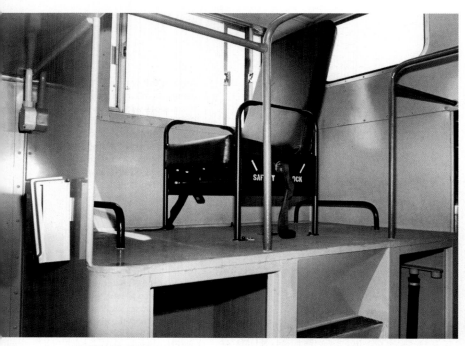

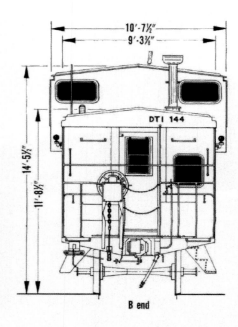

B end

By the 1960s, safety was strongly emphasized for caboose interiors. The padded, reversible chair in the cupola has a safety belt; note the recessed steps, rounded corners, and safety railings in this 1974-built ICC wide-cupola caboose built for Detroit, Toledo & Ironton. *Jim Hediger*

still ordering cabooses were looking for ways to cut costs. The Missouri Pacific built 100 new bay window cars in 1977 (nos. 13715-13814), but with short bodies on long frames in the style of a transfer caboose. The Union Pacific followed with a new design for a shorter, lighter bay window car, based on the MoPac design. The UP's new C-11 class cars—100 of them—were built by International in 1979. The bodies are 24 feet long with long end platforms (they're 41'-8" over the couplers). The body itself is 8'-2" wide; 10'-7¾" over the bays. Similar cars were built by Fruit Growers Express for Louisville & Nashville (50) and Clinchfield (6 cars).

Wide-cupola cabooses

The bay window design was widely adopted by railroads from the 1940s onward, but many railroads stuck with cupola designs. The next advance in design was keeping the cupola for the above-train view it offered, but making it wider: extending it beyond the sides of the body to help crew members get a better side view of a train like a bay window.

The Chicago Great Western built what might be the first of these cabooses with a series of rather Frankensteinish rebuilds of old wood cars that were originally built by

Haskell & Barker in the 1880s and 1890s. During rebuilding in the 1930s, the CGW rebuilt the cupolas, making them wider than the bodies and extending them below the car's roof level. Several cars were converted, with many variations. Some remained in service into the 1960s.

The Monon claims to be the first to apply the idea to a modern steel car, although its version did not extend the cupola downward below the car's roof line—the extension was just to the cupola sides above the roof edge. Thrall built several for the Monon, delivering the first production cars in 1951.

The first order of 20 of what became regarded as the "standard" wide-cupola caboose, built by International Car Co., was delivered to Duluth, Missabe & Iron Range in 1952. The all-steel design has what is sometimes described as a "saddlebag" design, with the cupola wider than the body (9'-7" body and 10'-8" cupola) and extending down below the roof level several feet (to the floor level of the cupola chair). This makes it comfortable for the operator to sit in the cupola without having to lean outward at the window opening.

International called its cabooses "Extra-Wide Vision" or EWV cars; other common descriptors include wide-cupola, wide-vision,

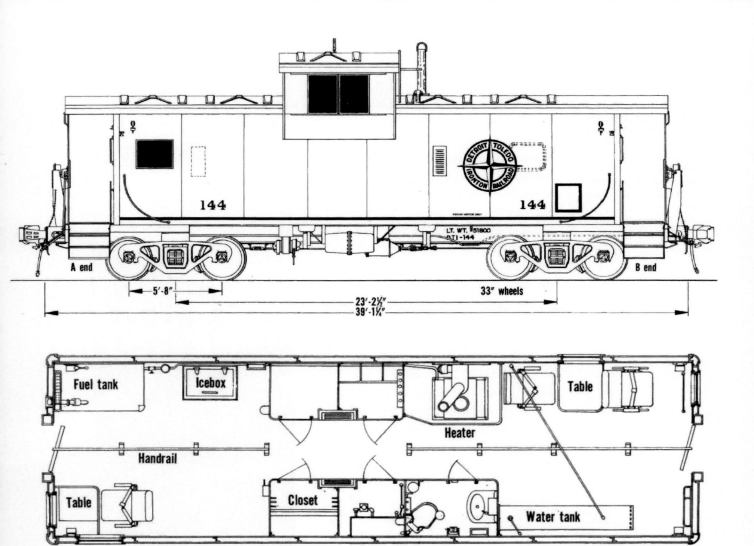

Labels on diagram: Fuel tank · Icebox · Table · Heater · Handrail · Table · Closet · Water tank

144 · 144 · A end · B end · 5'-8" · 33" wheels · 23'-2½" · 39'-1¼" · LT. WT. 51800 · DTI-144

or extended-vision cars. Whatever they are called, they became the epitome of the modern caboose, and were soon rolling on railroads across the country, but especially in the Midwest and West, where overhead clearance didn't present as many problems as with Eastern lines.

The wide-cupola caboose became the hallmark of ICC, and although other companies and railroads built them (see the list on page 142), ICC's were by far the most common. From the 1950s through 1981 International used the same modular construction methods as with their bay window and standard cupola designs to build thousands of EWV cupola cabooses, predominantly for Western, Midwestern and Southern roads.

The ICC EWV cabooses of various railroads have a similar look, but as with the company's bay window cars, the EWV cars are definitely not all the same: Each railroad prepares its own specifications, and these may vary from one order of cars to the next. The placement, number, and style of windows is the major spotting feature. Cupolas had two styles of end windows: wide and square. Other differences include trucks, marker lights, vents, and other details. International gets around the problems of individualized specifications by breaking the caboose design into modular units. Thus a caboose, made of standard panels that can be arranged into any desired combination of windows, louvers, and hardware, can be built according to the desires of the customer. The

International's wide-cupola caboose was a standard design, but many details varied among orders, including window style and placement, roof type (this shows a Stanray X-panel), cupola height, markers, and interior details and layout. Interiors also varied widely. This plan, for a Detroit, Toledo & Ironton order in 1974, lacks bunks and emphasizes seating. Toilets were standard equipment by the 1960s.
MODEL RAILROADER *magazine*

wide cupola is standard design, but it may be raised or lowered for clearance.

Some differences in cabooses tend to be regional. For instance, by the 1960s, railroads in the East tended to go easy on the number of windows and in providing sleeping quarters. (Most railroads by that time used rooming arrangements for their crews at nearby hotels.) In the West, where things were less populated (fewer rock throwers), the crews were more likely to stay in the cars, so windows can be more abundant and any sleeping arrangements are more elaborate.

Other differences among these cabooses were the roofs (diagonal panel, X-panel, or smooth panel) and running boards. Through the 1960s all had steel running boards and end ladders; after June 1970 most cars were built without them (per an Interstate Commerce Commission rule stating they "may be omitted"), and most were eventually removed from later cars, often with their supports left in place); and side sills (some had straight side sills; others had tabs/extensions over the ends of the bolsters and cross bearers in several patterns). Underframes varied; most were built on cushioned underframes from Darby or Waugh. They have the same shallow V-pattern end sills as ICC's bay window cars.

These are definitely modern cabooses compared to their predecessors built in the 1940s and earlier. Safety was a big selling feature for ICC's cabooses. All of the interior corners are rounded, steps are recessed into the walls (instead of projecting outward), and safety railings are placed around the stove and other hazards. An overhead railing runs along the center line of the ceiling. Table edges are padded and all doors and drawers are equipped with positive locking devices. Door and drawer handles are recessed.

There were several notable non-International wide-cupola cabooses as well. In 1966, Illinois Central built a series of wide-cupola cabooses at its Centralia, Ill., shops

Detroit & Toledo Shore Line no. 131 is a wide-cupola caboose built by International in 1972. It's at Durand, Mich., in October 1973.
Dennis Schmidt; Don Heimburger collection

(nos. 9650-9699), notable for their wide end porches (the cars were 42 feet long over end sills) with half-height walls next to the side walls. The railroad then turned to Darby for a series of nearly identical cars in 1968 (9500-9549; they had smooth instead of Stanray roofs). The IC then built another 100 cars in 1969 and 1972 (9550-9599, 9350-9399; the last with Pullman-Standard roofs).

Darby also built 10 wide-cupola cabooses for Missouri-Kansas-Texas in 1968 (nos. 125-134; they didn't have the large platforms of the IC cars). The Katy and the St. Louis-San Francisco built wide-cupola cabooses as

well, starting with earlier cabooses or boxcars (Frisco).

Perhaps the most unusual wide-cupola cars were groups of older cabooses rebuilt by International into wide-cupola cabooses for Gulf, Mobile & Ohio. The railroad had five former Western Maryland "Northeastern" cabooses that were refitted with ICC wide-vision cupolas in 1965 (nos. 2960-2964). Apparently pleased with them, the GM&O sent 40 former Alton cabooses (steel cars from the 1940s) to ICC, which rebuilt them with its wide cupolas. The results in both cases were distinctive, diminutive cars with

By 1992, when it was on a local at Mendota, Ill., Burlington Northern 12057 had its original side windows all plated over. It was built by ICC in 1975 without running boards or ladders. It has small cupola windows, tabbed side sills, and a built-in marker under the center of the eave. *Jeff Wilson*

Soo Line no. 72, built by International in 1973, lacks running boards and end ladders, has small end cupola windows, no side windows, and has a tabbed side sill. It's wearing the later maroon scheme at St. Paul in 1979. *John Luckfield; Don Heimburger collection*

Chessie System (Chesapeake & Ohio) no. 3322 was built by International in 1970. It lacks running boards and end ladders, has large windows on the cupola ends (with wipers), tabbed side sill, and small electric markers at each corner. The V-shaped end sill (painted yellow here) is apparent. *Chessie System*

Number 5703 is one of the first group of 60 wide-cupola International-built cars delivered to Seaboard Air Line (nos. 5700-5759). It has the wide style of cupola end windows. *Wiley M. Bryan*

large, modern-style extended cupolas.

Canadian National and Canadian Pacific each developed their own wide-cupola van designs. The first 150 CN cabooses were built in 1967 by Hawker Siddeley, and included a wide cupola centered on the body. The wide cupola, however, did not extend downward below the roof line. Better known are the railroad's Pointe St. Charles vans, 548 cars built at the PSC shops from 1970-1977. These used underframes and side panels from retired steel boxcars and had wide cupolas, were long (46 feet long over pulling faces)

with cupolas 10'-4¾" wide, and featured modern interiors including kitchenettes. Early versions had axle generators to charge batteries; later versions had propane-powered generators.

The Canadian Pacific began building wide-cupola cabooses at its Angus Shops (Montreal) in 1972, turning out more than 300 vans through 1981. The cupolas on the CP Angus vans were noticeably different than those on the Canadian National cars; the CN cupolas extended farther down the side of the body.

Santa Fe no. 999785 was among the final International cabooses built (in 1981), one of the 75 cars in class CE11 (999750-999824). Note the ladder grabs to the right of the cupola, the extended draft-gear box (for the cushion underframe), and built-in red marker. It's near Fort Worth, Texas, in September 1981. *Don Heimburger collection*

International built six EWV cabooses for Chicago & Illinois Midland (nos. 70-75) in 1972-1973. They lack running boards and ladders, have small cupola windows, and have amber rotating beacons atop the cupola. Number 72 is at Havana, Ill., in October 1977. *Glenn F. Monhart*

St. Louis-San Francisco no. 1205 was built by International in 1957 as no. 205. It's shown in August 1980. *Dick Wallin; Don Heimburger collection*

Duluth, Missabe & Iron Range wide-cupola caboose no. C-237 is from a 1974 order. It's at Proctor Yard (Duluth, Minn.) in October 1979.
Russ Porter; Don Heimburger collection

This is the caboose in the drawings on page 145. Number 143 is one of six (nos. 140-145) built for Detroit, Toledo & Ironton by International in 1974. It has a unique style of electric markers.
Jim Hediger

The conductor gives a friendly wave to the photographer as a St. Louis Southwestern freight rolls through McGregor, Texas, in May 1979. Number 23 is an example of an early ICC wide-cupola caboose, one of 25 (nos. 1-25) built for Cotton Belt in 1959. It's had its running boards removed (the supports are still in place).
Jim Hediger

Although built in 1981, National of Mexico no. 44429 was built with running boards and ladders. It has a straight side sill and wide cupola windows. It's at Aguascalientes, Mexico, in February 1992.
George Drury

Top: Illinois Central's Centralia Shops and Darby both built riveted wide-cupola cars for the IC. They had distinctive large end platforms, with half-height walls on the platform next to the body. Number 9377, built at Centralia in 1972, is at Rock Rapids, Iowa, in 1976. *Jeff Wilson*

Above: Number 9650 is from the first series of wide-cupola cabooses built at Centralia in 1966. It wears the IC's then-standard red scheme in its builder's photo.
Illinois Central

These vans were used on other Canadian lines as well, including Algoma Central (CN design), Ontario Northland (CP), and Toronto, Hamilton & Buffalo (CP).

Steel bay window and wide-cupola cabooses represented the apex of modern caboose design in North America. They were often the last cabooses operating as railroads began the move to reduce crew sizes and eliminate cabooses from trains through the 1990s.

St. Louis-San Francisco built several long-body wide-cupola cabooses in 1973, starting with Pullman-Standard PS-1 boxcar bodies. The cupola is off center and has a more steeply peaked roof than ICC cupola roofs. *Don Heimburger collection*

The Gulf, Mobile & Ohio's diminutive wide-cupola cars look like something a model railroader would kitbash—which is essentially what happened. Number 2960 is a former Western Maryland "Northeastern" style caboose (see Chapter 4) built in the late 1930s with a modern International wide cupola added to it. This technically shows Illinois Central Gulf action, as a month after the August 1972 merger a train rolls through Joliet, Ill. *Russ Porter; Don Heimburger collection*

Missouri-Kansas-Texas no. 209 is an International car that has been rebuilt with a shorter (lengthwise) cupola. It's bringing up the end of a train near Granger, Texas, in September 1980.
Don Heimburger collection

Canadian National's first 150 wide-cupola vans, built by Hawker-Siddeley in 1967, had wide cupolas that didn't extend down into the body. With icicles hanging over the roof, no. 79334 pauses at Windsor, Ont., on Jan. 2, 1981.
Jim Hediger

Canadian National's 548 Pointe St. Charles vans were rebuilt from older steel boxcars from 1970-1977. These were long—46 feet over couplers—and had wide cupolas of a different style compared to other WV cabooses. Number 78111, true to its "INTERNATIONAL SERVICE" stenciling, is at Pokegama, Wis., in August 1986.
Jim Hediger

The cupolas on Canadian Pacific's Angus Shops cabooses are more prominent and extend farther down the body than those on CN's PSC vans. Number 434426 is at Windsor, Ont., on New Year's Day 1981.
Jim Hediger

Chapter 6

Transfer cabooses,

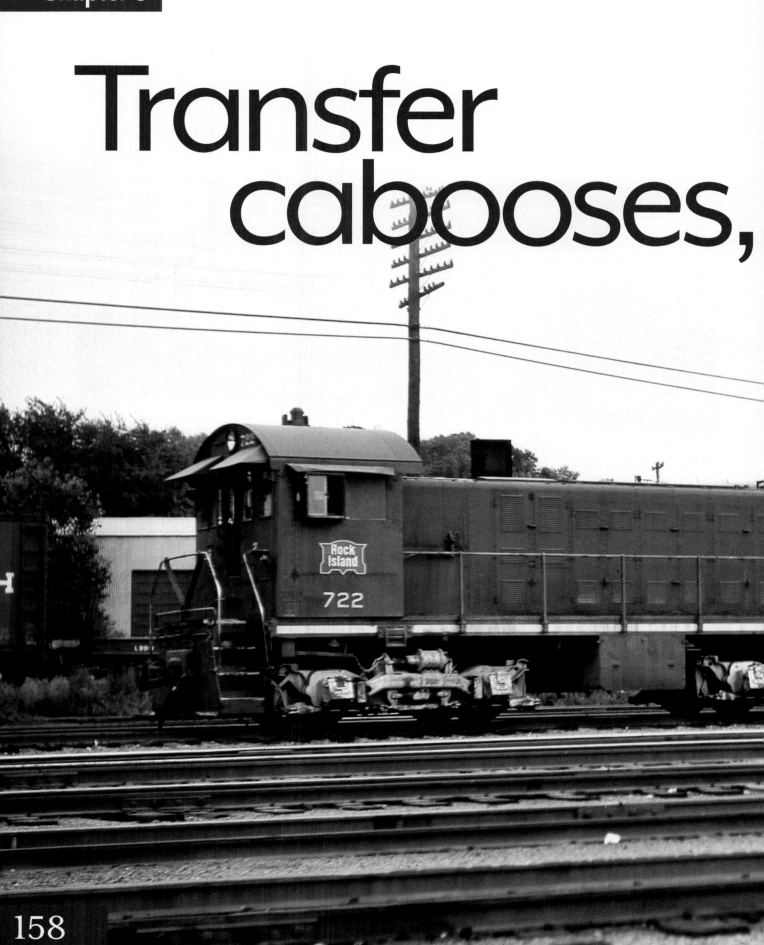

SPECIAL-SERVICE CARS WERE BUILT IN
A VARIETY OF SIZES AND STYLES

combines, & variations

A crew poses with Belt Railway of Chicago caboose no. 1 and 0-8-0 no. 141 sometime around 1920. The four-wheel caboose has a wood body with window built out from the side—an early forerunner to the bay window design. *M.D. McCarter collection*

Cabooses used in short-haul transfer service, as well as those used in branchline and mixed-train service, had distinctive appearances and features that set them apart from standard mainline cars. Many other cars resembled cabooses (or were sometimes rebuilt from older cabooses) including drovers' cars, business cars, bunk cars, and dynamometer and other test cars.

Transfer cabooses

Around major cities or industrial areas, railroads frequently shuttle large groups of cars from one yard and/or railroad to another. Runs typically are made to drop off cars, with the engine and caboose returning "light" (or "caboose hop"), with no cars. These movements are known as transfers. They've always required a caboose for rear-end crewmen, but since runs are short and speeds are slow, many features of standard mainline cabooses (cupola, bay windows, bunks, toilets) aren't needed or required. In fact, the ongoing need for transfer and local-freight operations (which sometimes require a rear platform for switching and complex reverse moves) is the only reason railroads retain any cabooses at all. The cars that serve these operations are known as transfer or yard cabooses.

Transfer cabooses fall into a couple of basic categories. Many look like a standard caboose, but without cupola or bay windows. Some of these were built this way, but many were rebuilt from older cabooses, with their cupola, bay windows, and any extra windows

Top: Belt Railway of Chicago had 30 short transfer cabooses of this basic design, with a riveted steel body, two windows on each side, and no cupola or bay windows. Number 212 is in Chicago in August 1977. *Russ Porter; Don Heimburger collection*

Above: Indiana Harbor Belt no. 123 is a wood-sheathed transfer caboose with sliding screens over both side windows. It's shown here in October 1970. *Russ Porter; Don Heimburger collection*

Above: Transfer caboose interiors tended to be more spartan than road cabooses. This wood Indiana Harbor Belt caboose in 1943 lacks stacked bunks and a cupola, but still has a corner desk, requisite air gauge and valve, ample seating, and a coal stove.
Jack Delano,
Library of Congress

Above middle: Great Northern rebuilt several of its older circa-1910s and 1920s 25-foot wood cabooses, removing the cupolas for transfer service. Some survived the Burlington Northern merger, including BN 10927 at Superior, Wis., in September 1974.
Bob's Photo;
Don Heimburger collection

Above right: Elgin, Joliet & Eastern transfer caboose 133 is at North Chicago in 1963. The freshly reconditioned car has a wood-sheathed body, heavy C-channel side sills, rides on archbar trucks, and has received permanent markers on each end (note red lenses on body). *Russ Porter;*
Don Heimburger collection

(all points where leaks often occur, or any extra glass subject to vandalism) removed. Inside, they've had bunks and other non-needed features removed.

The second style is the transfer caboose with extended platforms at each end. These are basically a flatcar or long frame with a shack or enclosure built in the middle. Many have been built new, and many others were rebuilt from older cars on flatcar or other freight-car frames (the Milwaukee Road built several on old frames from retired steam locomotive tenders; the Great Northern built a few on retired Baldwin diesel locomotive frames, even retaining the trucks). A key is simple construction—these cars were built with as few materials as possible and were designed to require as little maintenance as necessary.

Both styles vary widely in appearance and details, as many are one-of-a-kind or limited-run creations by railroad shops. Wood cars were common in early days, with steel more common after World War II. Platform-style cars were more likely to be steel, but some were wood.

The interior fittings are the basic difference between a transfer or yard caboose and a regular road caboose. Exactly what

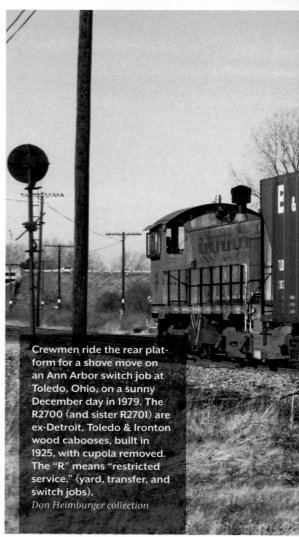

Crewmen ride the rear platform for a shove move on an Ann Arbor switch job at Toledo, Ohio, on a sunny December day in 1979. The R2700 (and sister R2701) are ex-Detroit, Toledo & Ironton wood cabooses, built in 1925, with cupola removed. The "R" means "restricted service," (yard, transfer, and switch jobs).
Don Heimburger collection

Santa Fe no. 999923 is a class CA-5 car that was rebuilt without a cupola in 1972, and spent most of its time at Chicago's Corwith Yard in transfer service. It retains one screen-covered side window (all windows on the other side are plated over). It's at Corwith in May 1981. *Jim Hediger*

items were required in each type of caboose was dictated by government regulations and the individual railroad's union agreements with its operating employees. In general, transfer cabooses had rather spartan interiors as they served primarily as a shelter for the trainmen working on yard or crosstown transfer jobs. Typical items included a desk or table, a couple of benches or chairs, a stove (coal or oil), a few steel lockers (bring your own lock), and little else.

Combines and side-door cabooses

Mixed trains were common on branch and secondary lines through the 1930s. Just as the title implies, a mixed train includes both freight and passengers. Most of the time that meant that an ancient wooden coach or coach-baggage car brought up the rear of a local, or "way" freight train. However, many

branchline mixed trains through the steam and early diesel era hosted only an occasional passenger or two—not enough to justify a standard passenger car. Since railroads in most cases were still legally required to provide passenger service, the solution to economically carrying a few passengers was the combine or stretched caboose, which simply had a few coach style seats added for passengers.

Along with passengers, another staple service provided by railroads through those eras was express parcel service (as part of Railway Express Agency) and standard railroad less-than-carload (LCL). In the days before United Parcel Service and FedEx dominated the industry, it was railroads through REA and their own LCL services that shipped and delivered parcels of all sizes for businesses and individuals. Along

Boston & Albany (New York Central) no. 1271 is an older wood caboose that's just been rebuilt without a cupola. It's in transfer service at Beacon Park Yard (Boston) in June 1946. *New York Central*

The Terminal Railroad Association of St. Louis had several short steel transfer cabooses built in 1944. They had tabbed side sills, steel panel roofs, and two windows on each side. Number 575 is at Madison, Ill., in May 1955. *Henry E. Bender Jr. collection*

Baltimore & Ohio Chicago Terminal owned this wood-sheathed, steel-frame transfer caboose. It has been freshly repainted and is at Chicago on Sept. 25, 1966. *Robert Stonich collection*

Union Pacific subsidiary Los Angeles & Salt Lake built five wood single-sheathed (steel-end), steel-frame transfer cabooses in 1955-1956 (nos. 3300-3304). They were renumbered UP 25917-25921 in the early 1960s. Number 3303 is at the Omaha, Neb., stockyards in 1961. *Merk Hobson*

Rock Island had several cabooses rebuilt from old single-sheathed boxcars, including some without cupolas for transfer service. Number 19165 was assigned to the yard at Cline, Kan., in 1971. *Don Heimburger collection*

Wabash built one-of-a-kind platform-style transfer caboose 02300 from an old 40-foot box-car. It's at North Kansas City in January 1965. *Charles E. Winters; Don Heimburger collection*

Norfolk & Western class R-1 transfer cabooses have wide steel-channel side sills and a steel body with windows on opposite corners and angled overhangs on each end. Number 518760 was repainted in 1974.
Bob's Photo; Don Heimburger collection

Erie Lackawanna built 25 transfer cabooses (T20-T34) in the late 1960s to a very similar pattern as the N&W caboose above, but without the wide C-channel sill. They have wood plank decks. Number T30 was assigned to Croxton, N.J., in the early 1970s.
Don Heimburger collection

Another railroad converting boxcars to transfer cabooses was Gulf, Mobile & Ohio. Number 2973, shown here in June 1978, is one of 16 (2970-2985) cabooses built in 1968 using frames from old 40-foot boxcars (and a caboose), with the body supplied by International Car Co.
Dennis Schmidt collection

mainline routes, this was handled by baggage cars in passenger trains (express) and boxcars (LCL) that dropped off parcels to railroad stations and freight houses.

On branch lines and many secondary and short lines, however, traffic levels didn't warrant full baggage cars or freight cars. It was left to crews of mixed and local freight trains to make these deliveries and pickups, often using the caboose to do so. For this service, railroads operated a wide variety of cabooses with freight ("baggage") compartments and side doors, which made it easier to load and unload parcels at station and freight-house platforms. Some of these

cars simply looked like standard cabooses with a small side door added. Others were much longer, with larger doors. Some stretched to 50 or 60 feet to allow ample storage space; many also included passenger seats for mixed train service as well. All were unique to the railroads that operated them. A few were steel, but most were wood cars; some were modified by railroads' shops from older cabooses or passenger cars, with bodies stretched and interiors rearranged. Most were assigned to specific lines and routes (and indeed had been built/modified for specific service), and rarely wandered from these assignments.

Kansas City Southern had several short transfer cabooses that were about as basic as could be produced: short steel platform with a steel box atop, with a simple projecting window on each side. Built in 1967, no. 395 is at Kansas City in April 1988. *Jim Hediger*

The trucks are a giveaway to the heritage of this Great Northern transfer caboose. The railroad built it and three others (nos. X177-X180) in 1965 on the frames of retired Baldwin diesel switchers, keeping the trucks (sans traction motors).
Great Northern

Among the biggest classes of transfer cabooses was Penn Central's N9 (160 cars; 18195-18354) and N9E (40 cars; 18355-18394). The N9s were begun by New York Central and completed by PC after the 1968 merger; the N9Es had a different (6V) electrical system and were built by PC. Number 18259 is at Toledo, Ohio, in June 1976.
Dennis Schmidt;
Don Heimburger collection

The Peoria & Pekin Union operated several small platform-style steel transfer cabooses, including no. 209, here at Peoria, Ill., in July 1963. The railroad at one time served 14 railroads in the Peoria area. *Russ Porter; Don Heimburger collection*

Baltimore & Ohio built this one-of-a-kind transfer caboose from a 40-foot boxcar at its DuBois, Pa., shops in 1976. The only member of class C-28, no. C-3051 is at Dayton, Ohio, in March 1978. *Robert Hubler*

Termed a "luxury transfer van" by builder Canadian National, these cars have a modified bay window (narrow body) on one side only. The railroad's Pointe St. Charles Shops built 200 of them (nos. 76500-76699) for transfer and terminal service in 1977-1978; no. 76539 is at Clarkson, Ont., in May 1978. *Kevin Holland*

Transfer cabooses are the main type of caboose that has remained in operation. Chicago Rail Link steel caboose no. 8 has been freshly repainted in this February 1990 scene; it rides on solid-bearing trucks that have been converted to roller bearings. *A. Stanisovaitis; Don Heimburger collection*

The Santa Fe in 1942 rebuilt no. 2312 from a drovers' car (built in 1931) to a coach/baggage/caboose car for branchline service. It was one of five such conversions (nos. 2310-2314). The car mainly served Kansas branch lines through the 1950s.
Bill Raia collection

Southern Pacific no. 475 was built by Pullman in 1911 as a Railway Post Office car for Houston & Texas Central. It was eventually rebuilt by SP in 1956 as a combination RPO-baggage-caboose. The 40-foot car, shown here in South San Francisco in 1966, rides on T-section cast freight car trucks. It was retired in 1972. *Henry E. Bender Jr.; Don Heimburger collection*

A Great Western train rolls by the depot at Eaton, Colo., in March 1948. The station platform is at the proper height to enable easy transfer of parcels with side-door caboose 1007. *Henry E. Bender Jr. collection*

The Chicago, Burlington & Quincy had several cabooses (waycars to the Q) rebuilt from passenger cars. Number 3973 was one of four class CW-7 ("combine waycar") cars (3971-3973, 3984). It measured 49 feet long, and was a combination coach-baggage-caboose for branchline service.
Paul H. Damrin

St. Louis-San Francisco built wood-sheathed no. 1150 at its Springfield (Mo.) shops in 1946 as no. 103. It has a sliding side door and 8-foot baggage compartment in the end opposite the cupola. Its plywood sheathing is still holding up in this mid-1970s view.
M.D. McCarter;
Don Heimburger collection

This wood-sheathed Cotton Belt baggage-caboose has a separate baggage (freight) compartment between the cupola and end of the car, with sliding doors on either side. *M.D. McCarter; Don Heimburger collection*

St. Louis Southwestern's long cabooses, such as no. 2304, included a baggage/freight compartment as well as passenger coach seating (windows at right) for mixed train service, mainly on the railroad's branches in Arkansas and Missouri. It's on train 160—a former mixed train—leaving Malden, Mo., in June 1961.
Steve Patterson

S.S.W.
2304

COTTON BELT

Burlington wood side-door caboose no. 14151 was built in 1889 at Plattsmouth, Neb., by predecessor Burlington & Missouri River, and it's still rolling in Sterling, Colo., in 1969 (and would survive several years into Burlington Northern). It's riding on Allied Full-Cushion trucks, which had been banned from interchange service in 1956. *Henry E. Bender Jr. collection*

Starting in 1937, Western Pacific built more than 40 cupola cabooses from old single-sheathed boxcars, including one, no. 403, which was built in 1937 with a baggage compartment and coach seats for mixed-train service. It's shown here in April 1939; it was reassigned to freight service in 1951 and renumbered 619.
W.C. Whittaker

California short line Santa Maria Valley used side-door caboose no. 170 for LCL (less-than-carload) and express service. The railroad acquired the car from the Union Pacific in 1926; it's working here behind a GE 70-tonner on May 8, 1956. The caboose was retired in 1962 (and is now restored and on display at the Oceano, Calif., depot). *Bob's Photo; Don Heimburger collection*

Great Northern built this stretched caboose in 1953 for branchline service. The 50-foot steel car had a long baggage compartment at one end. Nicknamed the "Hutch Caboose" for its usual assignment on GN's branch to Hutchinson, Minn., the car was built as no. X100 and renumbered X181 in 1966. *Russ Porter; Don Heimburger collection*

Some railroads converted LCL cabooses from old boxcars, or—in the case of Bangor & Aroostook; Detroit & Mackinac; Western Maryland, and others—from surplus World War II troop sleepers. These cars had side steps, grab irons, marker light brackets, and ladders added to follow regulations, with a couple of windows, an interior desk, bunks, chairs, and stove. They were most-often used on local freights on secondary lines to provide parcel and express service.

Branchline mixed-train and passenger service were common into the 1930s, but after that autos and trucks began cutting into business and many low-traffic lines were abandoned or services cut back. After World War II, growing airline service and the increase in good paved roads cut into all types of railroad passenger service; with it, railroad express and LCL service began a

The Missouri Pacific had a few steel side-door cabooses without cupolas. Number 1160, here in the early 1970s, was also fitted with a bay window. *M.D. McCarter; Don Heimburger collection*

Several railroads converted wood boxcars to basic cabooses, including the Georgia Railroad. Number 2839 was one of several rebuilt from single-sheathed cars. It kept its Murphy steel ends, with platforms and platform steps added inside them. It has end-ladder extensions, a rear brake valve, and marker light brackets. It's at Camak, Ga., in October 1967. *Dennis Schmidt collection*

Santa Fe converted more than 150 old single-sheathed boxcars to war-emergency cabooses in the early 1940s to handle increased trains and traffic. Windows, side doors, steps, and grab irons were added. Note the open-air benches atop the car in lieu of a cupola. *R.B. Miller*

The Monon built four cars in 1945 and 1946 in its Lafayette shops as "head-end cabooses," designed to handle LCL shipments on local freights. Rebuilt from old steel gondolas, they were originally numbered C-211 to C-214 and later renumbered 81211-81214. Number 81214 is at Hammond, Ind., in August 1971. *Dennis Schmidt; Don Heimburger collection*

Baltimore & Ohio converted an old steel boxcar to a caboose for local freight service. Number XM904 has new windows, side doors, steps, grab irons, and marker brackets. It's carrying the markers (small steel flags) for a local freight at Columbus, Ohio, on Jan. 5, 1965. *Dave Bunge*

Western Maryland converted this surplus troop sleeper to a caboose, removing the steam and signal lines and adding side and end ladders, running board, grab irons, side steps, and marker brackets. Inside, six bunks were left for crew use and a conductor's table added. Number 3060 is at Thurmond, Md., in July 1948. *Warren E. Olt*

Detroit & Mackinac initially converted this troop sleeper to a baggage car. The railroad then rebuilt it to a caboose after passenger service ended in 1951. Number 201 is at Alabaster Junction, Mich., in April 1963; it rides on its original Allied Full Cushion trucks.
Ray W. Buhrmaster;
Don Heimburger collection

Drovers' cars provided passage for the ranch hands and cowboys accompanying stock shipments. Santa Fe D936 is one of 10 steel 47-foot drovers' cars (D930-D939) built at the railroad's Cleburne shops in 1931. Most were eventually rebuilt to combines with side doors. This view is from August 1966. *Chris Burritt; Don Heimburger collection*

steep decline. This meant the retirement of most of these unique combine and waycar cabooses by the 1950s and 1960s.

A few mixed trains lasted longer—the Georgia Railroad's mixed trains between Atlanta and Augusta, Ga., made it until 1983—but they were the exception, not the rule.

Drover cars

Through the 1950s livestock was a major traffic source, particularly for railroads in the West, Midwest, and plains states. Especially during the fall, railroads operated full stock trains (or large cuts of cars) from small towns and rural areas to large union stockyards in major cities (Chicago, Kansas City, Fort Worth, Denver, Omaha, and others). Because cattle (and sheep and pigs) were limited in the time they could be aboard stock cars, these trains were given priority service.

To handle livestock en route, as when they had to be unloaded and reloaded for feeding and watering, owners of large shipments sent their own employees to handle them. They were known as drovers.

Chicago & North Western no. 10824 is one of several drovers' cars built in 1909 and rebuilt by the railroad in 1937, with cupolas removed and steel frames added. The wood-sheathed cars had lower seats that could be converted to bunks, with fold-down upper berths. The car is at Chicago's Proviso Yard in November 1952. The card tacked below the number says "RETURN TO BOONE IOWA." *Henry E. Bender Jr. collection*

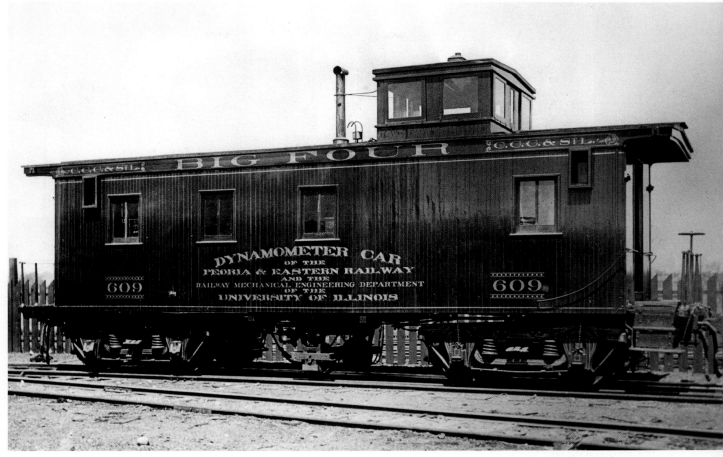

Railroads provided riding space aboard trains, usually in what became known as drovers' cars. These were sometimes built new for the purpose, but many drovers' cars were rebuilt cabooses or passenger cars with bunks and seats added. Drovers would sometimes be accommodated in standard cabooses if a drover's car wasn't available or if there were only one or two on a trip, but railroad crews hated this—drovers tended to take on the odor of their charges, and no rear-end crew member wanted their living space fouled in this manner.

Western roads operated the most drovers' cars: Chicago & North Western; Chicago, Burlington & Quincy; Santa Fe; and Union Pacific all had large numbers of these cars. As stock shipments declined rapidly in the 1950s, their need disappeared; most were gone by the 1960s.

Dynamometer and test cars

Dynamometer cars were in use by the late 1800s. These cars measure and record locomotive performance by calculating the strain load on the coupler, factoring in the weight of the train and the speed. They are invaluable in measuring locomotive power and efficiency (coal or other fuel usage) and in determining tonnage ratings, especially on specific grades. Among better-known early cars were those sponsored by the University of Illinois' Railway Mechanical Engineering Department. The testing and measurement equipment was housed in caboose-like cars of the Illinois Central and Peoria & Eastern.

As technology improved, dynamometer cars evolved and many railroads invested in cars (and railroads without cars regularly hired cars and crews from those railroads that had them). By the 1930s, most

University of Illinois' first dynamometer test car was no. 609, built by the Peoria & Eastern in 1898 and equipped by the university. It could check both track telemetry and train/locomotive dynamic forces. It was returned to use as a caboose shortly after the turn of the century when the school upgraded the test equipment in a different car.
Don Heimburger collection

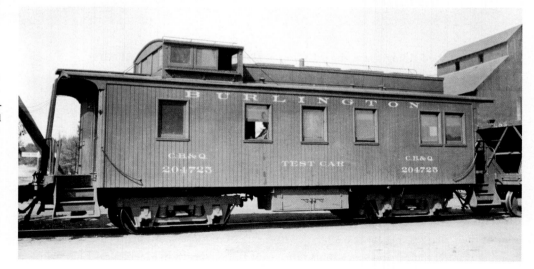

Illinois Central built U of I dynamometer car no. 17 in 1900, and the university equipped it with upgraded equipment compared to its earlier car (no. 609). The school rebuilt no. 17 with new equipment in 1907, including an auxiliary two-wheel truck to record speed (to the right of the left truck). The car is shown here with its crew during a break in testing at Mattoon, Ill., in May 1916. *University of Illinois*

Chicago, Burlington & Quincy no. 204725 is a dynamometer car rebuilt in a 30-foot wood caboose body from the railroad's earlier dynamometer car in 1901. It's shown testing locomotives on subsidiary Colorado & Southern in 1912; it served until it was replaced by an all-new car in 1929. *TRAINS magazine collection*

dynamometer cars more closely resembled passenger cars than cabooses, but most had a cupola-style observation bay atop the roof. On these cars, interior space was often provided for crew living quarters (bunks, lockers, small kitchen areas) as well as testing equipment.

A modern variation is TTX's test car, operated and staffed by its engineering and research department. The car, a former Illinois Central wide-cupola caboose, houses a variety of equipment for testing efficiency and rolling qualities of various TTX freight cars.

From the 1920s onward, dynamometer cars more closely resembled passenger cars than cabooses, although they retained cupolas. Burlington no. 30, built at its Aurora shops, replaced the railroad's earlier car in 1929. Testing equipment was to the right of the side door; crew living quarters to the left. *J. David Ingles collection*

Santa Fe dynamometer car no. 29 resembled a branch line stretched caboose. It served the railroad from 1912 until 1962. There's lots of railroad brass on hand as the car tests new Alco PA no. 51 as it carries the *Fast Mail* westward in October 1946.

Bob's Photo; Don Heimburger collection

Canadian Pacific no. 400494 looks like a caboose, but is a flanger, with a plow fitted under the carbody for removing snow. It lacks open end platforms, and the cupola is for the operator to better see the track during plowing. It's shown here in the early 1950s. *Bill Carruthers*

TTX bought a former Illinois Central wide-cupola caboose (a riveted car built at IC's Centralia Shops) and outfitted it with test equipment. It serves as a rolling lab, traveling with the company's intermodal equipment. *M.D. McCarter; Don Heimburger collection*

Other caboose-like cars

Cabooses were often converted to other uses. Bunk cars, used on work trains, were common. Another use was as an instruction car and business or office car: Although passenger cars were most often used for this service, a converted caboose provided a lower-budget alternative.

Old cabooses were sometimes rebuilt and put to work in snowplow service, either as control cars for large plows or outfitted with below-body plow blades in flanger service.

In these, the operator sat in the cupola and had to be alert to lineside flanger posts (the ubiquitous small angled black flag on a post that indicated a grade crossing or other between-rails obstruction) to raise the flanger blades to avoid damage.

Contractors acquired out-of-service cabooses to accompany their equipment. Common examples are rail-grinding services Loram and Speno. Chapter 8 shows a few additional examples.

Most railroad business and office cars are passenger cars, but Milwaukee Road converted a former steel cupola caboose (drovers' car) built in 1929 (from the railroad's first order of steel cabooses) first to an instruction car, then to a superintendent's office car. Number X5001 is at Bensenville, Ill., in December 1977. *T. Tancula*

Old cabooses were sometimes converted to bunk cars or crew cars to transport and house workers, often on maintenance-of-way crews. The Milwaukee Road converted one of their old rib-side welded bay window cars for this service; no. 980501 is at Savanna, Ill., in 1980. *Joe Moth; Don Heimburger collection*

Chapter 7

Rear-end crewmen did far more than ride the caboose and observe their train and the scenery rolling by. Here, as required by Rule 99, Illinois Central rear brakeman Ralph Canty walks back from the caboose to protect the rear of symbol freight MB-2, which has stopped on the main track near New Athens, Ill., in December 1955. Canty is carrying a red flag in his right hand and a fusee (flare) in his left. The conductor is walking forward, inspecting the left side of the train. *Wayne Leeman*

Caboose

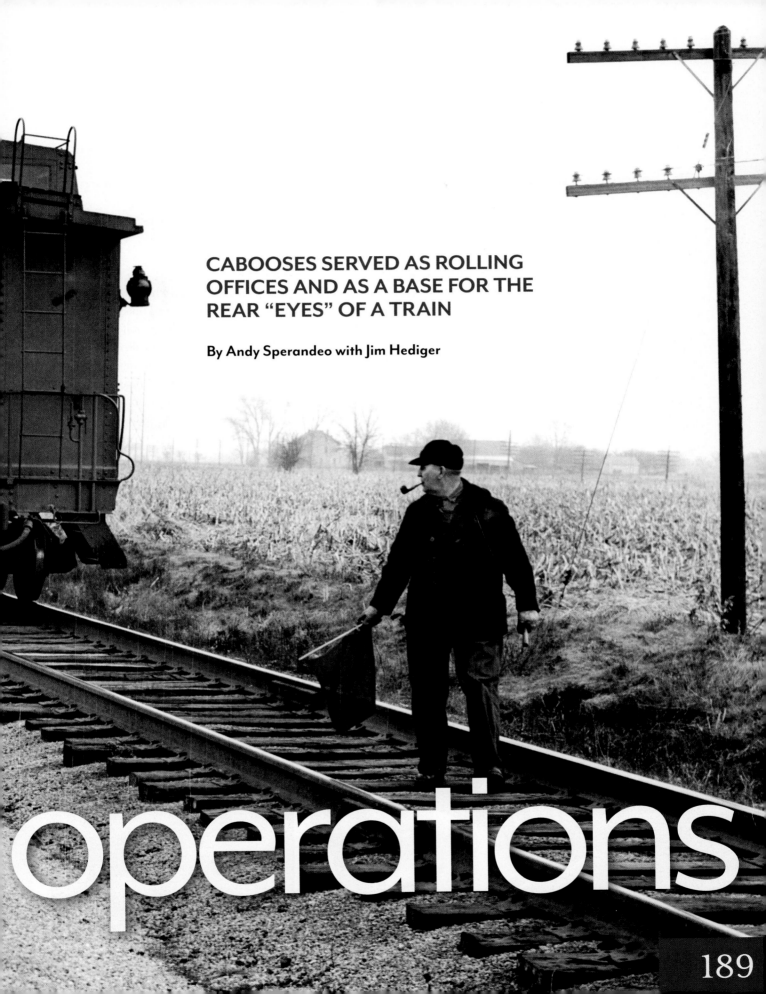

CABOOSES SERVED AS ROLLING
OFFICES AND AS A BASE FOR THE
REAR "EYES" OF A TRAIN

By Andy Sperandeo with Jim Hediger

operations

The caboose was far more than just the car that rode along at the end of every freight train. For more than a century, cabooses were a key center of train operations. The caboose served as a shelter at the rear of the train for the conductor and flagman/brakeman, an observation post allowing them to keep watch on their consist, an office for the conductor, and a rolling storehouse for tools and equipment.

As Chapter 1 showed, each caboose had a pressure gauge to monitor the train's air brakes, and a brake valve for emergencies. Some cabooses had combined air whistles and brake valves on the end platforms for signalling and braking during backup movements. By the 1940s, many cabooses began to carry two-way radios, allowing conversations en route with the engine crew (eliminating the need for many whistle signals) as well as wayside stations and interlocking towers.

Caboose crew sizes varied by era, railroad, and type of operation. In the steam era, the conductor (in charge of the train) used the caboose as his office, where he worked on all the paperwork (waybills and train lists) required for the train. He shared the space with a rear brakeman, whose job was to align switches, couple and uncouple cars as needed, and inspect the train if necessary (a head-end brakeman was also part of the crew, but rode up ahead on the engine with the engineer and fireman). Rear-end crews also often included a flagman, whose job was to protect the rear of the train when it was stopped while occupying the main line (more on that in a bit).

Assigned cabooses

Through the steam era, cabooses were outfitted with bunks, and cabooses sometimes served as living quarters at the train crew's away-from-home terminal. During this time, cabooses were typically assigned to crews (specifically to a

Picking up orders 'on the fly'

The first major step toward accident reduction occurred on September 22, 1851. A telegraph line was being strung adjacent to the Erie's right-of-way just seven years after its invention in 1844 by Samuel Morse. The westbound *Day Express* carrying Erie superintendent Minot stopped at Harriman, N.Y., for a scheduled meet, but the opposing train was late. In a flash of inspiration, Minot telegraphed the next office up the line, ordering it to "hold the (opposing) train for further orders." This was repeated at each station until the trains actually met at Port Jervis, N.Y., some 41 miles farther west. A new way of dispatching and changing previously issued schedules was born.

As telegraphic dispatching grew, it became standard operating procedure for the engine and caboose crews to receive orders at stations. There were two types of orders. A "31" order required stopping so the conductor could read it back to the agent, then sign it. A "19" order could be picked up "on the fly," while the train was in motion. (The 31 order was not used by all railroads.) The operator at a station would set the train order board (signal) to red (yellow in some cases) to let the crew know there were orders to pick up.

To hand up orders on the fly, the "flimsy" was written in triplicate on thin carbon-backed tissue paper. One copy went to the engineer, one to the conductor, and the agent retained one. The engineer's copy was tied in a string, which was tied across the top of a hoop-shaped wooden holder. Held aloft by the operator next to the track, a locomotive crew member stuck his arm through the hoop, grabbed the order, and tossed the hoop back to the ground for the operator to retrieve. An identical operation occurred as the caboose passed.

The hoop was first supplemented, then largely replaced with a Y-shaped holder. A string was tied around the train order, and tied across the Y-opening. As the train passed, the crewman grabbed only the order and tie string while the handle remained firmly in the operator's grasp. Permanent train-order racks were eventually placed at some locations, relieving the operator of the duty of handing up orders.

The operator at Chicago, Burlington & Quincy's Mendota, Ill., tower is about to hoop up orders to the conductor of a westbound time freight in 1954. The Y-shaped order hoop has string tied across the ends that hold the flimsies. The caboose is a new NE-12 steel car; the tower guards the railroad's crossing with the Illinois Central. *Philip R. Hastings*

The Burlington brake-man is on the ground to uncouple the stock car in front of the caboose after the switcher shoved it to the spot at the cattle pen. It's August 1955, and the brakie's cowboy hat is fitting for the Wyoming scene. The caboose is year-old NE-12 steel way-car no. 13526. *W.A. Akin*

conductor). This continued fairly late in the game, into the mid-1960s on many roads, even if crews no longer overnighted aboard them at terminals (this was typically required in work-rules agreements that railroads were obliged to follow). As an example, on the Santa Fe, pooling became allowed on its Coast Lines in 1957, but not until 1966 on all lines, which finally allowed cabooses to run through from Chicago to California.

An assigned car was used only when its crew or conductor was working, so a lot of cars had to be stored between trips. Every yard had a few unassigned cars that were available if a regular caboose was bad-ordered for repairs. On smaller railroads, cabooses were often assigned to conductors on a seniority basis, and they held onto their assigned cars as long as desired. When newer cars came along, the conductors bid on them and the senior man won out. The car he released then changed hands in the same way—a bidding process that could take months to get through a large seniority list.

Cabooses also had a table with seats, a stove and sink, drinking water tank, icebox,

and (by the late steam era) a toilet. Living aboard gradually became less common by the early diesel era, but a few crews still did so well into the 1950s, especially when laying over at outlying terminals.

During the wood-to-steel transition, some old-timers preferred wooden cars and looked upon the newer "tin boxes" with disdain. An occasional specific caboose might be blacklisted for a variety of reasons, including accident history or an unlucky number!

Switching cabooses on and off trains at crew-change points was a necessary operation for years. Crews worked on districts (or subdivisions) of 100 miles or more, and long-distance trains required several crews to reach their destination. When cabooses were assigned to crews, every time the crew changed, the old crew's assigned caboose was switched off the train and the new crew's caboose put on. Even if the locomotive(s) and all cars in the train were going through, there was still some work for a yard engine in swapping out cabooses. And, since this changed the train's consist, a standing brake test was required.

Division or specific assignments were often stenciled on the side of the caboose (usually below the number). Variations included train number assignments. As the move to non-crew-assigned cabooses grew, railroads often specified certain cabooses as "pool" cabooses. This was indicated with stenciling, specific numbers, or subletters (Burlington Northern and Union Pacific, for example, labeled pool cabooses with a big "P").

Servicing

Yards at division points and other key locations had one or more "caboose tracks" assigned to store and service cabooses. When crews lived aboard the cabooses at "away" terminals, these tracks were usually placed in a quiet location away from the noise of the yard or engine terminal. Separate double-ended tracks held the cabooses from each division working into the yard. This allowed cabooses to be easily switched on the same first-in, first-out basis used to call the crews. A yard switcher placed the inbound car on one end of the track, and the departure yard engine could easily pull a caboose from the opposite end.

Crew callers let the yardmaster know when a crew or conductor had accepted a call to work so the appropriate caboose could be added to the train. Switch crews handled cabooses gently to avoid disturbing sleeping occupants. Note that switch engines moved the cabooses between the caboose track and the trains. The practice of using an entire train as a "handle" to pick up or drop off a caboose is strictly a model railroad move.

Each caboose was serviced between

A brakeman rides the rear platform of one of Reading's International Car Co. wide-cupola cabooses. The electric markers are on, displaying red to the rear, as the train heads into a yard. *Don Heimburger collection*

The caboose tracks at Louisville & Nashville's Decoursey Yard at Latonia, Ky., held cabooses of L&N as well as run-through cabooses from Conrail and Detroit, Toledo & Ironton (cupola on track at right) in June 1980. The concrete platform improved access for servicing. *Jim Hediger*

The caboose track was a staple of every division-point yard. Here eight wooden Soo Line cabooses—from freshly painted to weathered—wait on the ready track at North Fond du Lac, Wis., in April 1964. *Russ Porter*

trips, but the exact procedures varied with the number of cars handled at a terminal. Arriving cabooses were given an initial mechanical inspection, and the conductor turned in a condition report, noting any needed repairs. Newer cars had their fuel and water tanks filled and the toilet's retention tank emptied; older cars had their coal bins filled. The truck journal bearings (for solid-bearing trucks) were checked and oil was added if needed.

Interior cleaning followed, including trash removal, mopping the floor, and window washing, then an electrical inspection and radio check (beginning in the 1950s on most railroads). Supplies of consumable items like paper towels, toilet paper, and printed forms were restocked, and the car's racks of fusees and flagging equipment were checked and refilled as needed.

Crews usually cleaned their own assigned cabooses, so they had an incentive to keep the car clean—and they were generally spotless. Even so, most of the dirty work went to the lowest-seniority crewman. Supplies were kept nearby so the junior man could restock anything that was needed.

Whenever more trains ran in one direction than the other, even occasionally, railroads might run short of cabooses at one end of the subdivision. Railroads tried to anticipate this and balance cabooses just as they do with locomotives. In anticipation of a westbound weekend rush, for example, a few eastbound trains at the end of the week could have two or more cabooses.

Only the rear car of a multi-caboose train necessarily carried a working crew, however. Depending upon traffic and available trains, additional crews, paid to "deadhead" to the other end of the district, might ride a passenger train on their passes.

Regular runs such as a five-day-a-week way (local) freight often attracted high-

A near disaster

When the conductor "pulls the air" on the engineer, it often is looked upon by the head end as meddling. But not always. On one occasion, an engineer almost wanted to kiss me (the conductor) for pulling the air. It's impossible to say what would have been the outcome of this incident—I don't mean the kissing part—but one day I found it necessary to stop my train by utilizing the conductor's valve in the cupola of the caboose.

This bizarre incident occurred on the Hoxie Subdivision of the Missouri Pacific's Arkansas Division, involving CFZ, a Chicago-Fort Worth expedited train powered by three six-axle diesel locomotives. Luckily for all concerned, we had a little red caboose on the rear of the train, not some automated device. Running the authorized 60 mph, we approached a yellow signal, which warned us that the next signal would be red. Suddenly the engineer found himself helpless to control the speed of his train because of a unique air-brake failure.

I had taken charge of the train at Poplar Bluff, Mo., for the 179-mile run to North Little Rock, Ark. My rear brakeman and I were riding in the caboose. Bill Bailey, the head brakeman, and Jessie Johnson, the engineer, were in the lead unit. During our trip Jessie had set and released the brakes numerous times, and we had no indication that we might have an air-brake failure. Shortly after we passed the dragging equipment/hotbox detector south of Tuckerman, Ark., I felt slack action in the train, as the coupler of our caboose slammed up against the one on the car ahead. I gave the air gauge a quick glance, looking for some indication that the engineer was setting the air brakes. According to the reading of the gauge, he was not making a brake reduction, so I dismissed the slack from my mind.

Seconds later the engineer came on the radio with a message that might sound perplexing to some outsiders, but would be well understood to Hoxie Sub trainmen: "Let me know when the caboose stops, Bill."

I gave the caboose air gauge another quick glance. It was sitting on 80 pounds, and I did not feel the brakes setting on the train. A request like this is usually made by the head-end crew when there has been an emergency application of the air brakes, and our caboose air gauge gave me no indication that this had happened.

"Are you in emergency?" I asked Jessie.

"Have been for the past half-mile, and we are not slowing down," came the reply.

Years of training took over. I pulled the conductor's valve open and "dumped the air" in the train line, putting the brakes on the train into emergency, then braced myself for possible slack action as I felt the train starting to stop. After the train stopped, the rear brakeman and I started walking to the head end, giving each car an inspection for a possible defect. Up ahead I could see the engineer and head brakeman standing at the rear of the third unit.

"What's wrong?" I asked the head-end crew.

"The brakes went into emergency just before we reached the approach signal, but we were not slowing down," said Jessie, who was visibly shaken.

"Did you pull the air?" head brakie Bailey asked me.

"Yes," I replied.

"And a good thing you did. See what happened," Bailey said as he pointed to the space between the third unit and the head car.

Bailey had called my attention to an almost unbelievable sight. The train line (air pipe) on the car behind the engine had broken away from its mooring and had dropped low enough that it struck a crosstie and bent double. The mishap caused the air hoses to separate, putting the three diesels into emergency. The train line, however, had bent so quickly that none of the air inside it had escaped, keeping the

Missouri Pacific brakeman Joe Adams is on the radio telephone in the cupola of a caboose on hotshot perishable Train 62, carrying lettuce in October 1952. The phone, air gauge (at right), and brake valve were all vital pieces of equipment. *Wayne Leeman*

brakes from applying on the rest of the train.

Feeling his locomotives go into emergency and thinking the rest of the train had followed suit, Jessie bailed off the engine brakes to keep the diesels' wheels from sliding. But when Jessie realized the train was not reducing speed and saw the red signal up ahead with a train stopped in the block, he called me on the radio to inform me that something was terribly wrong. Luckily for all concerned, the radio on the caboose was in working order and Jessie informed me that he was running wild. I would hate to think what the net results would have been if I had not been informed that our train was running out of control. As you can see, this was a near disaster.—*William Church*

Through the 1950s, when cabooses were assigned to specific conductors, cabooses were switched on and off of trains at every crew-change point. This was done by a switching locomotive, in this case a Santa Fe 2-6-2 at Canadian, Texas, in March 1943. The devices on the front of each cupola are "highballers," used to signal the head-end in pre-radio days. *Jack Delano, Library of Congress*

seniority crews because of the regular hours. Their cabooses in effect became "assigned" to those trains and were thus subtracted from the pool available for through trains.

Pool and run-through cabooses

As you can imagine, the crew system meant railroads needed a *lot* of cabooses to cover crews plus have extras on hand. Efforts to improve train speeds and reduce operating costs in the mid-1950s led to changes in union agreements to allow some cabooses to be used in pools. Within a decade, systemwide pool agreements required new or upgraded standardized cabooses that had full electrical and water systems, oil heat, polycarbonate window glazing, radios, refrigerators, retention toilets, high-backed seats, and roller bearings.

Pool cabooses operated across division boundaries, so crew changes were reduced to the time it took one crew to step off and the next one to climb aboard.

By the 1960s, run-through freights among two or more railroads were becoming common. In many cases the locomotives ran through for the entire trip; cabooses sometimes did the same. When doing so, cabooses had to be equipped to match regulations, radio specifications, and union agreements for all railroads involved. Foreign-road cabooses would be serviced at the home railroad's end terminal before making the return journey.

Helpers and cabooses

Helper or pusher operations—adding a locomotive to a train for part of its run to "help" it climb a steeper grade than on the rest of the line—was (and still is) a common operation on many railroads. Before today's radio-controlled distributed power units (DPUs), those added locomotives had their own crews who worked as a team with the road engine crews to get trains over the railroad's Big Hill. Railroads used many

On Union Pacific, the big "P" on the cupola denoted a caboose in pool service (as opposed to being assigned to a specific conductor). Number 25546 is one of 100 class CA-8 cabooses built for UP by International in 1964. It's shown here at Kansas City in 1985. *Jim Hediger*

A Lehigh Valley conductor and rear brakeman stow their grips aboard a Norfolk & Western pool/run-through caboose at Buffalo, N.Y. The train is the last run of the *Apollo*, a run-through intermodal train being handed off from N&W to LV. It's March 31, 1976; Conrail will assume LV operations the following day. *Ken Kraemer*

Two steel cabooses of differing styles trail a Clinchfield train in Family Lines paint. If more trains run in one direction than another, cabooses (and sometimes crews) need to be shuttled back in the other direction. *Don Heimburger collection*

techniques to do this, with the goal to do it safely but also to do it in a timely manner, with a minimum of individual switching operations to keep trains moving.

Double-heading—adding the helper in front of the road engine—was the simplest way to add power to a train. This was most often done through the steam era on passenger trains, which were comparatively lightweight, but was sometimes done on freights too. However, too much power applied at the head end might exceed the strength of freight-car draft gear.

Adding a pusher at the rear of a train was the most common arrangement with freight trains. Pushers reduce the strain on draft gear, since the drawbars toward the rear of the train are in compression instead of tension.

With cabooses, the question was always whether the pusher could be added behind the cabin or if it must be placed ahead of it. Operations were much simpler if the pusher could be behind the caboose, but individual railroads had their own rules and policies; often the deciding factor was whether the

caboose had a steel underframe to transmit the pusher's power. There were also laws in a few states requiring pushers of a given weight or tractive effort to be ahead of occupied cabooses. Either way, the train is stopped at the base of the grade before adding the pusher.

If the pusher is ahead of the caboose, the train must stop at the summit and some kind of switching maneuver, possibly involving a gravity "drop" from an inclined track, is needed to cut the pusher out of the train and get the caboose back on. Then the train needs to make a standing set-and-release brake test, which it may need to do anyway if it will be descending a steep grade on the other side of a mountain.

If the pusher is behind the caboose, operations become simpler because it's possible to cut it off while the train is in motion ("on the fly"). There's drama in dropping a pusher on the fly. Railroads did this with a long valve handle on the rear caboose platform to close the angle cock on the brake pipe, as well as a chain or extension

Railroading goes on day and night in all weather. It's 11:55 p.m. on a snowy Feb. 2, 1960, and a switcher (left) has just tacked the caboose onto a Pennsylvania Railroad TrucTrain piggyback train. The conductor gives the highball to the head end with a fusee; he'll soon be on his way eastward. The caboose is a classic PRR N5 steel car built in 1916, entering its sixth decade of service. *Don Wood*

A way of life

The railroad is a dirty, dangerous place to work, and the successful start of every journey aboard a caboose carried with it the prospect of an uncertain end. For every dozen trips completed without incident, there were a few untold others marked by vicious storms, pulled drawbars, derailments, encounters with hobos, and myriad other contretemps. Shifting loads, engine failures, grade-crossing accidents, and delays caused by other trains could make for a long day. In the worst winter weather—those days when even regular wavers didn't appear at their windows or trackside posts—a few minutes spent flagging in a blinding blizzard could make a man compose love songs to a No. 14 Sun Beam Railway Cabin Car Stove as he strained to hear four shouts from a distant whistle, relieving him of his dreary post.

Still, "the other side of the job," as railroaders called return journeys, brought balance to what outsiders saw as a vagabond existence, and enforcement of the Hours of Service law lessened the week-long caboose encampments that marked the industry's early years.

For all its frustrations and hardships, life aboard cabooses forged a common bond. Over time, trainmen of the 1,001-caboose Chicago, Milwaukee, St. Paul & Pacific and the one-crummy Gainesville & Northwestern came to realize their occupational kinship with conductors and brakemen of such distant pikes as the Bangor & Aroostook, Atlantic Coast Line, Gulf, Mobile & Ohio, and Sacramento Northern, developing an oft-times fierce pride in their calling and their respective companies. A New York Central conductor once told me he regularly tossed inoperative lanterns from his caboose as it crossed the highest bridge on his division, not from anger or distaste but because he and his colleagues felt the schedules of their busy railroad and the safety of its employees couldn't be compromised by faulty equipment.

Once indoctrinated, few men of the caboose turned away. "I'd be there yet if they'd let me," John Bragg told *Smithsonian* of the railroad his peers referred to as the "Best & Only." "Hell, they had to drag me off."—*William Benning Stewart*

Three Rock Island cabooses—a single-sheathed cupola car sandwiched between a pair of 1964-built International bay window cars—roll at the end of a westbound freight at Pullman Junction, Ill., in 1968. *Russ Porter; Don Heimburger collection*

Missouri Pacific brakeman Roy Brooks and conductor B.P. Simpson couple a helper locomotive to the rear of a wood (steel-frame) caboose near Rolla, Mo., in October 1942. The train (the second section of No. 34), with 66 cars and 3,300 tons, will soon be on its way eastward to St. Louis. *Wayne Leeman*

lever to pull the uncoupling lever and lift the coupler pin, uncoupling the caboose from the pusher. The pusher's brakes then set automatically when the air hoses separated, and the train continued on its way.

Operating rules treat pushers as part of the train they're helping. The helper crews receive copies of all the clearances, train orders, or track warrants delivered to the train while they're helping it. Once cut off from a train, a helper locomotive needs independent authority to return to its base. Typically it runs as an extra train displaying white classification signals and rear-end markers.

Flag protection

One of the oldest safety practices in railroading is flag protection for trains or engines occupying main tracks. The photo on page 188 shows how it was done in the classic era, although signal and communication systems in today's cabooseless era now sometimes allow train crews to be relieved of the requirement by specific timetable or bulletin instructions.

For most of the 20th century, flag protection was generally prescribed by Rule 99 in each railroad's book of operating rules. A widely used version of this rule reads, in part:

The Santa Fe opted to cut its pusher locomotives in ahead of the steel caboose on this freight climbing Summit at Cajon Pass, Calif., in 1979. Number 999455 is a radial-roof product of the class CE-2 rebuild program, one of 233 turned out in 1969-1970. *Don Heimburger collection*

"When a train stops under circumstances in which it may be overtaken by another train, the flagman must go back immediately with flagman's signals a sufficient distance to insure full protection, placing two torpedoes (explosive noisemakers that detonate under wheels) and, when necessary, in addition, displaying lighted fusees (flares). When recalled and safety to the train will permit, he may return, leaving the torpedoes and a lighted fusee."

The operational benefits of flagging rules might not be apparent if you think only of unexpected stops on the main line. But flag protection also allows for more convenient use of the main line. For example, a crew could leave most of the consist of a way freight on the main line under flag protection while the engine takes just the cars to be worked into town and has the passing siding free for running around.

Or say a train is tucked into a siding for a meet but the locomotive is in a spur on the other side of the main line making a setout. The timetable says the opposing second-class train is due, but the conductor knows it's running late and the crew only needs about five minutes to pull out of the spur and back into the siding. By sending out a flagman to protect the movement, the locomotive can go ahead and use the main safely, then recall the flag when the engine is clear.

The Northern Pacific was fine with having 2-8-2 no. 1647 give a push directly behind wood-body caboose 1777 at Duluth in August 1957. Tractive effort was sometimes the determining factor in whether to cut pushers in ahead of a caboose.
Russ Porter

A steel Southern Pacific caboose carries the markers behind GS-1 4-8-4 pushing a drag freight eastbound east of Tucson, Ariz., in 1953. Caboose 1354 is a class C-30 car, one of 180 built from 1947-1951.
Robert Knoll

"Recall the flag"? We'll get to that and other whistle signals shortly. And notice that the train dispatcher doesn't have to be involved in any of the above operations. Except in Centralized Traffic Control territory, under the regime of Rule 261, train and engine crews don't need the dispatcher's "track and time" or "work time" authority to use the main. It's up to the crew of each train to know when they can safely use the main track, and flag protection makes that easier.

Whistle signals

Most communication among train crews today is by radio, or by standardized hand signals when operators are within sight on the ground. Before radio became common, railroads used whistle signals for communication between the head end and caboose or among locomotives (between the head-end locomotive and a helper engine, for example).

Railroad operating rules define the specific signals to be used. In most rule books from the steam/diesel transition era, this information is contained in Rule 14, "Engine Whistle Signals." Rule 14 is too long to quote here, but here are some common whistle signals.

An example is the most common signal used, one that even many non-railroaders know: Rule 14(l), when approaching a "public crossing at grade"—a street, road, or highway crossing—signal with two long sounds, a short sound, and finish with one long sound. This is usually written out as

Weather was always a hazard for train operations, particularly on cabooses. Here section hands shovel out a snowbound Denver & Rio Grande Western narrow-gauge train in the Animas Canyon. Number 0573 is a short-body wood two-truck caboose.
John Norwood collection

Inspecting other moving trains was a key duty for caboose crew members. Here a Great Northern brakeman, his train in a siding, is on the ground behind his wood caboose to give the *Empire Builder* a once-over by Cut Bank, Mont. *Philip R. Hastings*

During backup moves, the conductor can apply the train brakes using a brake valve ("back-up valve") on the caboose's rear platform. Switching moves like this are why some cabooses are still in use. This is on the Montana Rail Link at Livingston, Mont., in January 2014. Caboose no. 1004 is a former Burlington Northern car. *Len Torney*

Missouri Pacific conductor C.S. Woodworth tosses a bundle of waybills to yard clerk Sam Stefo as his train rolls under the Chouteau Avenue overpass entering St. Louis in August 1975. The train is symbol freight KSI from Kansas City; the caboose is a wide-cupola design built by International.
Wayne Leeman

The operator at Gilman, Ill., hands up box dinners to the caboose crew of a southbound Illinois Central Gulf freight in September 1980.
Donald J. Krofta

This Missouri Pacific caboose was on a stopped train when it was struck from behind by another train at Webster Groves, Mo., in May 1973. Crew members were shaken up, but not seriously injured. *Wayne Leeman*

A dangerous ride

Its charm and heritage notwithstanding, the caboose—essentially a box on wheels, perforated with openings and filled with obstacles for its occupants—was an inherently dangerous vehicle to board and ride. Caboose lore is filled with stories of smashups, injuries, and deaths brought about by short flagging, overlooked meeting points, switching errors, derailments, and train break-in-twos. Rear-end collisions were a leading cause of premature retirement for cabooses, but an overturned oil lamp could quickly incinerate a wooden car and a track washout could spell doom for even the sturdiest steel crummy.

At the start of the rear-end trainman's workday, rolling thunder from the head end announced that the hogger was flexing every muscle of the iron horse to stretch the dozens or even hundreds of feet of slack which reposed in the drawbars of a motionless train. Slack could throw a man from a platform or cupola, smash him into bulkheads and tables, and break enough bones to abbreviate his career at an early age. The problem was exacerbated at speed when slack ran in and out

on grades, hobbling a conductor's pen on his wheel report at best, bringing him considerable bodily harm at worst.

Equally dreaded was the urgent hiss of the train air going into emergency, a sudden, darkly ominous prelude to unfolding and potentially grievous events. For the men of the caboose, the longitudinal, ceiling-mounted handhold installed aboard most waycars was not an appliance of mere convenience.

Cabooses improved in style and comfort over the years, but the conditions that typically brought them and their riders to grief remained. In addition to the potential disability or death of trained and tenured employees, the destruction of a modern steel caboose whether through wreck, fire, or grade-crossing accident could represent a loss in excess of $70,000. As time and technology began to revamp traditional railroading, management came to see the caboose as a high-cost, high-risk anachronism from another era, one kept alive largely through prevailing laws and labor agreements.—*William Benning Stewart*

a sequence of dashes and zeros, so this signal looks like "— — o —." The rule also says that the last sound is to be prolonged until the crossing is reached, or if necessary repeated.

For any crewman on or near a train, it's vital to know signal 14(b), "— —" (two long sounds), meaning "release brakes, proceed." This announces that the signaling train is about to start. It's part of getting a train under way, almost a ritual, and "whistling off," as it's called, is vital to let other crew members (particularly those on board the caboose, or about to board the caboose) that the train will soon be in motion. Signals are subject to interpretation by engineers, and often 14(b)'s long sounds get shortened to a couple of staccato blasts. Sometimes it can

sound almost casual; at other times, like a drill sergeant's word of command.

When a train has to stop unexpectedly and may be overtaken, signal 14(c), "— o o o," tells the flagman to protect the rear of the train. This is called "whistling out the flag." (There's no signal for protecting the front of the train; the head brakeman is already on the engine if protection against opposing movements is needed.)

When it's time to recall the flagman, there are two signals used to prevent confusion in case multiple trains are in the area. Signal 14(d), "— — — —," means "flagman may return from west or south," while 14 (e), "— — — — —," recalls the flagman from the east or north.

The boy on the wheelbarrow at right is transfixed by the passing train, and the conductor and brakeman are out of the caboose as a Great Northern freight rolls through Hancock, Minn., in the 1940s.
Great Northern

Chapter 8

Descent

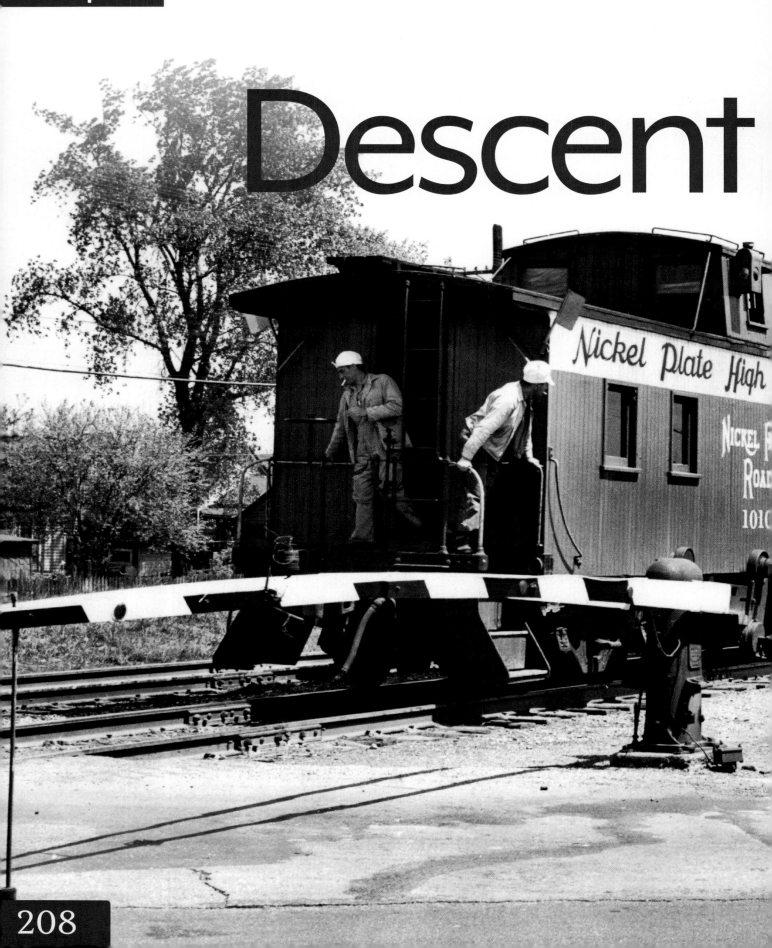

CABOOSES REACHED THEIR TECHNOLOGICAL PEAK JUST WHEN THEY WERE NO LONGER NEEDED

into history

As wonderful as this 1949 scene is to look at—from what many consider the glory days of railroading—most elements within it are long since technologically obsolete: the classic automobiles, the manually operated crossing gate (which required a full-time operator), and yes, the caboose, with its two or three crewman who kept an eye on the brake pressure and the train ahead. The classic Nickel Plate Road wood caboose, with conductor and brakeman on the rear platform, brings up the markers for a freight rolling through Hammond, Ind., in 1949. *A.C. Kalmbach*

Modern cabooses of the 1970s and '80s—such as this 1981-built Missouri Pacific bay window platform road caboose—were technologically advanced, but even with shortened bodies and "old" features such as cupola and bunks stripped away, they came with healthy price tags ($60,000 to $70,000). Operating them, including the price of the crew members, added additional expenses.
Bob's Photo; Don Heimburger collection

While the caboose's Golden Age rolled on in the 1970s, the dark side to the multiple improvements found on newer designs materialized. They all cost money—substantial money—and the railroad industry was in a downward spiral. Many older cabooses were in poor condition. By 1975 a new caboose could cost $70,000 or more, with all its mandated and standard equipment. By 1980, with a recession looming, it was claimed that the cost to update or replace the entire U.S. caboose fleet would approach $1 billion.

Many older cabooses remained in service in the 1980s, including this 1940s-era Milwaukee Road welded caboose in 1983. Many had been converted to local or transfer service (as "shoving platforms"), with windows plated over and most internal features stripped away.
Don Heimburger collection

This Burlington Northern (former Northern Pacific) International wide-cupola caboose was state of the art when built in 1969, but is looking faded and a bit worse for wear at St. Louis in 1991. By this point, cabooses were being retired in large numbers.
Don Heimburger collection

Inflation was rampant; many railroads serving the Northeast were in bankruptcy and continuing to lose money. Cabooses were an expense railroads wanted to minimize, and preferably eliminate.

The railroads' initial response to rising costs was the creation of pool services. Locomotives and cabooses covering these assigned runs rolled through normal crew-change points and interchange connections from railroad to railroad, with only the crews, not the power or cabooses, changing. Run-through operations saved money and improved efficiency. However, when a dozen or more crews use a caboose during a single long trip, most of the housekeeping duties are left for the next

crew. By the end of the round trip, cabooses frequently were a mess. The era of crew personal pride was over.

Even more important, while significant money was being spent upgrading or buying new cabooses from the 1950s through the 1970s, technology was moving forward. The development of microwave-based radio technology alone provided vastly improved railroad communications. Between hand-held radios and expanding areas of Centralized Traffic Control (CTC) and automatic block signals, timetable-and-train-order operations were giving way to radio-issued track warrants, and the rear brakeman's job was being rendered obsolete on other than local or way freights.

Ultimately that self-same microwave signal delivered the *coup de grace* to the caboose. Hit by striking operating union crews in 1963, the Florida East Coast began operating trains with two-man crews (the national union agreement was three to five men) and no cabooses. As the strike continued (it lasted to 1971), the FEC engineering staff in 1969 produced a steel enclosure with an air-pressure transducer and microwave transmitter inside. It had an external flashing red light, was designed to mount in the rear car's coupler, and communicated to the locomotive via radio signal, essentially replacing the caboose and crew—the first end-of-train (EOT) device. By 1972, cabooses had run their last miles on the FEC.

However, the FEC was an intrastate, not interstate railroad. Thus, it was free of ICC regulation and able to try new technologies whereas interstate railroads could not. The Brotherhoods were furious, but legislative pressure could only slow, not stop, the coming revolution.

Union intransigence and full-crew laws postponed for a decade the widespread use of

End-of-train devices (EOTs or ETDs) come in many styles. Modern ("smart") EOTs monitor brake pressure, can receive commands from the head end, include a blinking red light, and are powered by siphoning a small amount air from the brake line to move a turbine to charge the battery.
Trains magazine collection

Coast to coast in cabooses

In retrospect, it is frustrating to realize that in riding from coast to coast in cabooses from 1936 to 1980, not once did it occur to me that I was sitting in the midst of a revolution affecting this type of equipment. Yet that certainly was the case. I was on board as wooden sides gave way to steel, kerosene lamps were replaced by electricity, hand signals lost favor to radio, and crummies in effect became steel palaces.

Oh, yes—at the outset, cabooses at most locations changed with each new crew. In at least three instances I rode with rear-end crews who slept in the caboose between runs: on the old Nickel Plate, the former Frisco, and the now defunct Arkansas & Ozarks. At one time this was anything but an unusual practice, particularly in the West.

How come personal caboose riding? As a metropolitan newspaper reporter with a lifelong interest in railroading, I was able to get permits to ride with promises of stories if details worked out. They usually did. Permits generally were good for engine or rear end. In many cases I took the latter because information about train make-up (waybills) and other facts were easier to come by in the caboose. In addition, on really long rides, it was by far more feasible to catch a few winks of sleep in the caboose. Once I survived 22 crew changes from California to Missouri in five days. Twice I followed a car of lettuce from Watsonville, Calif, to St. Louis. Another long one involved tracing crude rubber from unloading in New York City, moving to Akron, Ohio, for processing, and on to the West Coast.

I never encountered a hostile crew member. Occasionally one would make sure I wasn't in the process of generating a hatchet job on work rules. Otherwise, they all had one word of advice: Sit down when the train is moving to avoid getting knocked down by slack action. It never happened to me, but that slack action really could be something. Most rear-end crew members had horror stories about such a thing. I recall plenty of run-in and run-out on the old Missouri Pacific between Kansas City and Pueblo, Colo.

Above: The crew of an eastbound Santa Fe train gets a wave from a westbound crew member near Dawn, Texas, in March 1943. *Jack Delano, Library of Congress*

Left: The rear brakeman of a northbound Seaboard Air Line produce train is on the rear platform of his wood caboose to inspect a southbound merchandise train. The action is on SAL's double-track main line in the late 1940s. *Seaboard Air Line*

Since there often was plenty of time between movements at crew-change points, I often photographed the rear-end equipment. As I look back on that photographic record, it dramatizes the changes that took place even if I wasn't aware of it at the time.

It is ironic that the caboose became an endangered species just as caboose building reached a peak of achievement. It is also worth asking why railroads continued to turn out crummies in the 1970s and early 1980s when those newfangled, telemetric rear-end devices held out so much promise. A case in point

is Missouri Pacific before it was merged with Union Pacific. MoPac built 100 new transfer-style CA-11 cabooses in 1977 and another 150 in 1980 (see page 210). In 1977, the cost was up to $40,000 from $19,000 in 1970. All 250 were called short-bay models. Fittings included water cooler, ice chest, water tank, retention-type toilet, wash basin, oil-fired furnace, seats for three trainmen, radio, and writing boards for a desk. There was no provision for cooking or sleeping.

Compare all this with the "good old days." Things sure do change.—*Wayne Leeman (from* Trains, *August 1990)*

the end-of-train device. However, its use was codified in the 1982 United Transportation Union national agreement, and by the mid-1980s the caboose's retreat became a rout.

There were other considerations besides money. The shift to roller-bearing trucks greatly reduced the hazards of dry wheel bearings and the frequency of hotboxes. Remote hotbox and dragging-equipment detectors were more reliable in locating potential dangers than even the most experienced rear-end crew. And even the best, most-modern safety-appliance-equipped caboose still could not prevent the omnipresent presence and danger of slack, and slack was still a primary cause of crew injury. Undeniably, crews of cabooseless trains had fewer injuries.

The total number of cabooses peaked around 35,000 in the mid-1920s; by 1950 it was 25,000, and by 1970—thanks largely to pool (and run-through) arrangements and longer, less-frequent trains—14,000. The count was about 12,000 when the EOT floodgates opened in the early 1980s. By the 2000s, perhaps a few hundred remained active, nearly all in local and transfer service. In less time than it took the diesel to replace the steam locomotive, the EOT pushed the mainline caboose into the history books.

EOT devices

End-of-train devices (usually called EOTs or ETDs) have now been in nationwide use for more than four decades. Today, most EOTs look nearly identical to the ones that arrived in the early 1980s; however, the new ones are far more sophisticated and, in some cases, just downright smarter.

First-generation EOTs were comparatively simple devices. Powered by a rechargeable battery that would report the air pressure at the rear of the train to the head end, its other job was to keep flashing its red light from dusk to dawn as the marker for a normal yard-to-yard mainline

Axle ends on solid-bearing trucks—with their journal boxes that required constant oiling and repacking—were always a threat to overheat, and spotting the telltale smoke or fire from a dry bearing was a key reason for having eyes looking forward from the caboose. Their elimination in favor of roller bearings, together with the advent of dragging-equipment and hotbox detectors, eliminated much of the need for crews in cabooses. Here Santa Fe conductor E.K. Hill checks a bearing on a refrigerator car near Texico, N.Mex., in 1943. *Jack Delano, Library of Congress*

By the 1990s, long strings of cabooses awaited scrapping at many major yards. More than a dozen Norfolk & Western cabs, numbers crossed out, sit in a dead line at Wasena Yard at Roanoke, Va., in April 1994. *Roger Amato*

trip. A fresh battery from the radio shack, a quick inspection, and then it was back out on another train.

Most of today's models still have a battery, but increasingly it is used only as backup, with the EOTs' power self-generated by a small internal air turbine that steals a little air off the brake pipe to make its own electricity. Estimates suggest that 20 percent of the fleet by 2006 used a turbine, with more coming into service as older models are retired. A typical EOT that has had its share of drops, bounces, and thuds usually lasts a bit more than 5 years.

By the 2000s, "smart" EOTs were engaging in two-way communication. These devices can report brake pressure information to the head end, as well as receive a

command to apply emergency braking.

The Wabtec Railway Electronics model TrainLink ATX (there are other manufacturers) is topped with a rubber-encased antenna that both accepts and sends signals from and to the head end, with a smaller round black GPS module knob. Inside, just below and behind the red reflector, is a rechargeable backup battery capable of powering the EOT for at least 12 hours.

The EOT is securely clamped to the coupler of the last car, tightened down by turning clockwise the short black rod below the carrying handle. When snug, the black rod is attached to the handle with a clip so it won't work loose. On the bottom, the EOT is connected to the brake hose.

This classic former Pennsylvania Railroad class N5 caboose, built in 1923, is long removed from mainline freight trains but was still serving for Amtrak in maintenance-of-way service in the Northeast Corridor in the early 1990s. *M.D. McCarter; Don Heimburger collection*

The Department of Defense maintains a fleet of cabooses of various types. They provide shelter for guards and other personnel accompanying shipments. Former Rio Grande no. 01483 is at East St. Louis in February 1994. *Robert Stonich collection*

Loram rail grinding service uses this International bay window caboose as both a crew car and a firefighting car, putting out any small fires caused by the sparks from grinding. It was at Kennesaw, Ga., in August 1990. *Don Heimburger collection*

The Southern Pacific around 1990 outfitted several cabooses, including class C-50-9 car 4762, built in 1980, as "railroad police" cars. They carried agents aboard intermodal and auto rack trains that were prone to theft and vandalism. They have air conditioners and exterior spotlights.

TRAINS magazine collection

All this is useless, however, without the head-end crew being able to monitor the device. On older locomotives, a HOT (head-of-train) box is mounted atop the engineer's control stand (newer locomotives have an integrated HOT box). Along with a multi-line display showing the brake-pipe pressure at the rear of the train, these devices also have a switch on the front panel shielded by a red cover. If the train has to be put into emergency braking, pressing that button simultaneously activates the EOT to apply emergency braking from the rear, too.

Where cabooses went

As EOTs began taking over operations on a large scale in the mid to late 1980s, lines of stored cabooses began appearing at yards across the country. A select few of those in the best condition were kept for the few transfer, local, and switching jobs that still required a rear platform for crews. Some are still in service in the 2020s, and although many look quite worse for wear, some have been refurbished and repainted.

Most cabooses, however, were destined for the scrap line—including many that had barely put in 10 years of service. Others continued rolling in other services, including maintenance-of-way (including fire and plow service), as crew or control cars for services such as rail-grinding crews (including Loram and Speno), or off their trucks as yard offices and sheds.

Many cabooses found homes in public parks. Burlington Northern no. 11582—a former Northern Pacific wide-cupola caboose built by International—is on display at Centennial Park in Underwood, Minn.
Russ Porter

Top: A crew member prepares to step off a Columbus & Greenville freight at the retired caboose that serves as the yard office at West Point, Miss., in September 1981. *Louis Saillard*

Above: Cabooses of all vintages and railroads can be found at museums across the country. Many have been restored inside and out. Soo Line 99085, built in 1909, is on display at the Mid-Continent Railway Museum at North Freedom, Wis., in 1979. *Don Heimburger*

Museums large and small have acquired cabooses for display and preservation, and many still operate cabooses as part of regular excursion or on-site trains. Many have been restored to their original appearances.

Thousands of cabooses were purchased by private owners and trucked off line to serve as cabins, shops, or offices—caboose motels can still be found here and there across the country.

Across North America one is never far from a caboose, even if it's not bringing up the rear of a passing train. Few items of mid-19th century industry continue to exist, much less still serve us today, nearly 160 years after Nat Williams invented his "Conductor's Car." The Little Red Caboose continues on, as public space, private space, or simply as a pleasant reminder of railroading's past. That in itself is perhaps a full-time job for the 19th century caboose in 21st-century America.

Much of the section on end-of-train devices is from David Lustig's "End-of-train devices keep on evolving in back," published in the August 2006 Trains.

The hiss of a torch

Southern Pacific 4059, built by Pacific Car & Foundry in 1961, met the scrapper's torch in October 1989—a fate that befell thousands of cabooses of that period.
William T. Morgan

For decades, cabooses have punctuated the ends of trains. Now it seems the end of cabooses might not be far away. And for some the end is imminent. On October 3, 1989, I spent some time with cabooses whose days were numbered. It was an unusually cool day in Mojave, Calif., as I walked solemnly amid dozens of cabooses at the Purdy Company's railroad salvage yard. In past visits I had seen a few cabooses here, along with boxcars, flatcars, and other rolling stock. However, after an absence of about three years, I was surprised upon my return visit to see the landscape covered with row after row of cabooses. Most were Southern Pacific and Cotton Belt bay-window hacks, but some Santa Fe cupola cars also were present. Two rows of the doomed vehicles had been placed on the ground, with one row tilted over at a sharp angle. Cotton Belt 63 had been unceremoniously shoved off the end of track, breaking off one of the steps in the process. Some cabooses were marked "sold" or "save" in chalk, but the majority were destined for the scrapper's torch.

As I walked slowly down the rows, I couldn't help but imagine the places these cars had visited in their careers ... Cajon Pass, Tehachapi Loop, Raton Pass, San Diego, Kansas City, New Orleans. And, of course, they had all visited Mojave at least once. And what about the thousands of men (and probably some women) who rode in all those cabooses over the years? Imagine the happy times they spent, and the sad times. They endured the heat of desert summers and the frigid temperatures, fierce winds, and snow of mountain winters. Where are those railroaders now? Would any of them shed a tear if they could see this forlorn sight in the Mojave Desert?

A hissing sound brought me back to the present. I had wandered to the west side of the Purdy grounds; the sound was coming from an oxygen-propane torch being used to cut apart SP bay window caboose 4059. Two men, one at each end of the car, looking like visitors from another planet in their protective garments and hoods, quickly and methodically cut apart the veteran vehicle. The hiss of the torches and bright display of flying sparks added an unearthly touch to the somber scene. It took only a few minutes to cut out one side panel. The metal would be sliced into 18 x 36-inch (or so) pieces and be loaded into TPCX (The Purdy Company) gondolas for shipment to Geneva Steel in Utah, or to other companies.

After several minutes of watching and photographing the demise of SP 4059, I turned and walked slowly away, never looking back. Perhaps it was best to remember 4059 as it once was, instead of as a pile of metal plates scattered about the sandy soil. Later, as I drove from the company property, I paused for a last look. What a sad sight the doomed cars made as they lingered in the bright desert sun.—
William T. Morgan (from Trains, *August 1990)*